I0480256

ARTBOOKS

FROM CRESCENT MOON PUBLISHING

Leonardo da Vinci
by James Pearson

Early Netherlandish Painting
by Rosalind Mutter

Piero della Francesca
by Naomi Haskell

Giovanni Bellini
by Julia Davis

Eric Gill: Nuptials of God
by Anthony Hoyland

Minimal Art and Artists In the 1960s and After
by Laura Garrard

Postwar Art
by George Knighton

Vincent van Gogh: Visionary Landscapes
by Stuart Morris

Max Beckmann
by Stuart Morris

Egon Schiele: Sex and Death in Purple Stockings
by D. Simon Eade

Mark Rothko: The Art of Transcendence
by Julia Davis

Jasper Johns
by L.M. Poole

Brice Marden
by Laura Garrard

Frank Stella: American Abstract Artist
by James Pearson

Bellini
By Jennie Ellis Keysor

The Life of Michelangelo Buonarroti
By John Addington Symonds

Dante Gabriel Rossetti
By Esther Wood

Rodin: The Man and His Art
Edited by Judith Cladel

Rodin
By Rainer Maria Rilke

Fra Angelico
By James Mason

The Madonna In Art
By Estelle Hurll

The Venetian School of Painting
By Evelyn Phillipps

Boucher
By Haldane McFall

Leonardo da Vinci
By Maurice Brockwell

Famous European Painters
By Sarah Bolton

Delacroix
By Paul Konody

VERONESE

VERONESE

BY FRANÇOIS CRASTRE

TRANSLATED FROM THE FRENCH
BY FREDERIC TABER COOPER

CRESCENT MOON

First published 1912. This edition © 2023.

Set in Book Antiqua 10 on 14pt.
Designed by Radiance Graphics.

Images are used for information and research purposes, with no
infringement of copyright or rights intended.

Thanks to the authors and publishers quoted.

British Library Cataloguing in Publication data

ISBN-13 9781861716231

CRESCENT MOON PUBLISHING
P.O. Box 1312, Maidstone, Kent, ME14 5XU
Great Britain, www.crmoon.com

CONTENTS

NOTE ON THE TEXT

The text is from *Veronese* by Francois Crastre, translated by Freferic Taber Cooper, and published by Frederick A. Stokes Company, New York, 1912.

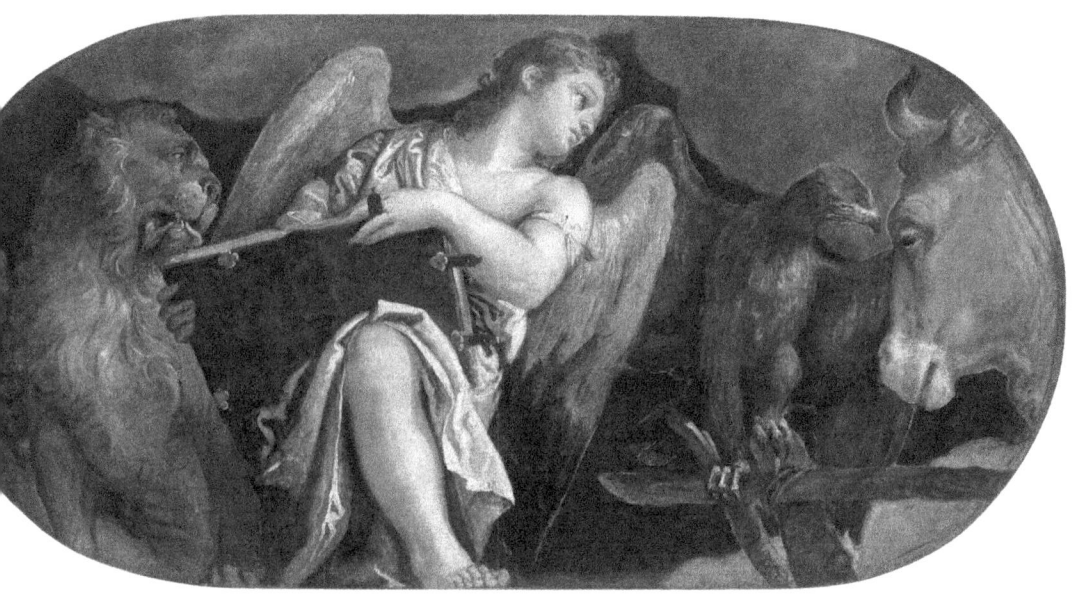

Paolo Veronese, The Symbols of the Four Evangelists

INTRODUCTION

It has been said of Veronese that he was the most absurd and the most adorable of the great painters. Paradoxical as it sounds, this judgment is perfectly true. Absurd, Veronese undoubtedly was, in his disdain of logic and common sense, in his complete indifference to historic truth and school traditions, and in his anachronistic habit of garbing antiquity in modern raiment. "I paint my pictures," he said, "without taking these matters into consideration, and I allow myself the same license which is granted to poets and to fools." And it is precisely his riotous fantasy, his naïve self-confidence, his own peculiar way of understanding mythology and religion that have made him the adorable artist whose glory has been consecrated by the centuries.

Thanks to the rare power of his genius, the most audacious improbabilities vanish beneath the magic adornments with which he covers them, and it hardly occurs to one to notice his glaring historical errors or the superficialities of his pictorial conceptions in the continual delight inspired by the sense of concentrated life in his characters, the splendour of his colouring, the caressing charm of his draperies, the brilliance of his skies, and the impression of youth and of joy that radiates from his work. Veronese was neither a thinker nor an historian, nor a moralist; he was quite simply a painter, but he was a very great one. If his preference is for the joyous scenes of life, that is because life treated him indulgently from his earliest years; if he delights in giving to his pictures a sumptuous setting, in which silk, brocades and precious vases abound, it is because he acquired a taste for these things in that matchless Venice of the sixteenth century, marvellous treasury of sun-bathed, gaily bedecked palaces, wherein all the opulence of the East had been brought together. What these paintings of Veronese reproduce for us are the thick, rich carpets of Smyrna, newly unladen from Musselman *feluccas*, monkeys imported from tropic islands, greyhounds brought from Asia, and negro pages purchased on the Riva dei Schiavoni, the Quay of the Slaves, to bear the trains of the patrician beauties of Venice. But, above all, one finds in them Venice herself, Venice the Glorious, queen of the sea, Venice sated with gold and lavish of it, sowing her lagunes broadcast with palaces, and the robes of her women with diamonds. More truly than Titian or Tintoretto, Veronese is the chosen painter of the Most Serene Republic. He not only decorated the ceilings of her palaces and the walls of her churches: but he took the city of his adoption as the setting for all his compositions; it is at Venice that the *Feast at the House of Simon the Pharisee*, the *Feast at the House of Levi* take place; it is in Venetian surroundings that Jesus presides over the *Wedding Feast at Cana*.

One can understand how the painters of the Venetian school, nurtured in the dazzling and joyous light of the sea-born city, transferred to their palette that vibrant colour with which their artist eyes were filled; nor is it surprising that Veronese, passionately enamoured of Venice, achieved, through his wish to glorify her, that magnificence of colour and of expression which remains his distinctive mark.

THE FIRST YEARS

Nevertheless, Veronese was not a native of Venice but of Verona, as is indicated by the surname that was bestowed upon him during his life and that has adhered to him ever since. His rightful name was Paolo Caliari. He was born at Verona in 1528 and not in 1530, as is asserted by several of his biographers, notably by Carlo Ridolfi. The correct date is now verified by the discovery, in San Samuele of Venice, Veronese's parish church, of the register of deaths wherein the decease of the great painter is entered as having occurred the 19th of April, 1588, the very day when he completed his sixtieth year.

Paolo Caliari belonged to a family of artists. His father, Gabriele Caliari, was a sculptor and enjoyed some little reputation in his own city. Veronese's uncle, Antonio Badile, was a painter, and in such pictures as are known to be his we find evidence not only of a good deal of ability, but of a certain facile grace that justifies the high esteem in which his compatriots held him.

Veronese's father, being of a logical turn of mind, wished, since he himself was a sculptor, to make a sculptor of his son. Veronese learned to model statuettes in clay, and, aided by his precocious intelligence, he acquired a real dexterity in this art, quite remarkable in one so young.

But this was not his vocation. Frequent visits to the studio of his uncle Badile had awakened in him an enthusiasm for painting. He applied himself to learn to paint with so much zeal and imagination that his father made no attempt to check his inclination, but entrusted him to Badile. The latter was Veronese's real teacher, though not the only one, for young "Paolino" also attended the studio of another Veronese painter, Giovanni Carotto.

From the outset, Veronese applied himself energetically to perfecting his skill in line drawing. The future genial painter of wondrous fantasy yielded himself without a murmur to the rude but salutary exigencies of technique. Strange caprice on the part of an artist who was destined to show so much dexterity in execution and lavishness in decoration, his tastes turned towards the most severe and least imaginative of masters, Albert Durer and Lucas Van Leyden. It was through copying the engravings of these illustrious masters that he learned how to draw. Such lessons always bear their fruit. In this laborious apprenticeship, Veronese acquired that steadiness of hand, that firmness of line that was later to be noted even in his most exuberant paintings, despite the enormous quantity of canvases that he produced in the course of his life.

Even his earliest attempts reveal his abundant and facile genius; and these first, and one might almost say immature, works already foreshadow the great artist. The affectionate patronage of his uncle Badile greatly facilitated his début. At an age when young folk have not usually begun to form dreams of the future, young Caliari had already forced himself upon the attention of Verona, and the Chapter of the Church of San Bernardino commissioned him to paint a Madonna.

He acquitted himself well of this task. The work proved satisfactory, other orders followed, and the name of the young artist swiftly spread beyond the confines of his native city. A short time later, the cardinal Ercole di Gonzaga decided to decorate the cathedral at Mantua, recently rebuilt by Giulio Romano. He sent a summons to Caliari, as well as to three other Veronese painters who enjoyed a big reputation: Battista del Moro, Paolo Farinato degli Uberti, and Brusasorci, who was regarded as the Titian of Verona. The cardinal instituted a sort of rivalry between these four artists, and gave them orders for four pictures, destined to be competitive. The subject entrusted to Paolo Caliari was a representation of the *Temptations of St. Anthony*. The young painter applied himself resolutely to the task. Far from intimidating him, the redoubtable competition of his three elders served only to excite his ardour and stimulate his imagination. He painted the saintly anchorite defending himself against the blows which the Devil is dealing him with a stick and repulsing the advances of a woman who has been raised up from hell itself to tempt him. The cardinal, delighted with this picture, gave preference to Veronese over his three competitors.

Veronese lost no time in returning to Verona, but, however flattering the esteem with which his compatriots surrounded him might be, he was not long in finding that the limited scope afforded by his native city was too narrow for his activity. He had a boyhood friend, Battista Zelotti, a painter like himself, and also like himself tormented by dreams of glory. Together they quitted Verona and betook themselves to Tiene, in the duchy of Vicenza. Here they had the good luck to meet a man of discrimination, in the person of the paymaster-general Portesco, who entrusted them with the decoration of his palace. The two friends apportioned the work between them; while Zelotti, who had studied at Venice under Titian, undertook the fresco painting, Veronese decorated the intervening panels in *grisaille*, or gray monochrome. The result of this friendly collaboration was a complete series of paintings, of great diversity: hunting scenes, banquets, dances and numerous subjects borrowed from mythology or from history, the *Loves of Venus and Vulcan*, the *Heroism of Mucius Scaevola*, the *Festival of Cleopatra*, and a remarkable *Sophonisba*. This work in common was not without profit to Veronese. Zelotti's manner closely resembled his own; they both show the same qualities of colouring and composition, and the same broad and facile touch.

They collaborated once again on fresco work in the home of a certain Eni, in the village of Fanzolo, in the neighbourhood of Trevise. After this they separated, Zelotti going to Vicenza, whither he had been summoned, while Caliari betook himself to Venice, the Promised Land towards which he was impelled by his ardent desire for glory.

When he arrived in the Most Serene Republic, Caliari was not yet twenty-five years old. We have no reliable document regarding these first years of his residence there, nor even of the impressions produced upon him by the opulent and magnificent city. But these impressions are easy to conceive. To anyone so sensitive as he to externals, Venice must have seemed enchanted ground. How could he have failed to be dazzled, in acquainting himself with that gorgeous city, enthroned upon the Adriatic, like a pearl in a casket of velvet? With what joyous eagerness his colour-enraptured eye must have rested upon those white marble palaces, moulded and filagreed in arabesque, those churches paved with precious mosaics, those quays swarming ceaselessly with a picturesque and motley crowd of Armenians, Greeks and Moors, spreading the sun-bathed pavements with a glittering display of spangled ornaments, turquoise-inlaid cutlery, and multicoloured fabrics.

If the models that passed in endless procession before his eyes impressed him as magnificent opportunities, the sight of what other painters had already wrought from this material aroused his artist soul to keen enthusiasm. The whole constellation of the great Venetians had converted the city of the Doges into an incomparable museum: Giorgione, with his melancholy compositions, full of vague dreams; Carpaccio, with his naïve and picturesque reproductions of Venetian life. Among the living, Sansovino, simultaneously architect and artist, who built marvellous palaces and adorned them with graceful frescoes; Tintoretto, sombre genius whose creative power largely redeemed the somewhat obscure tints of his palette; and above them all, Titian, the great Titian, who at that time was already eighty years of age, yet still manipulated his brush with the firm hand of youth.

All these masters Veronese admired indiscriminately, as was fitting in a young painter who had never known other models than those of his own small city. He ran the danger of acquiring mannerisms and becoming an imitator. By a special grace accorded to genius alone, Veronese succeeded in remaining himself and borrowing nothing either from his predecessors or his contemporaries. From his contemplation of the works of the others he gained only a nobler passion for his art; and he altered nothing in the personal vision which he already formed of men and of things.

Vigorous, blessed with good health, jovial by nature, and much enamoured of the bright and sparkling side of life, Veronese fashioned his paintings in the image of his own temperament. His work was always an exaltation of the joy of living, an apology for those agreeable externals that render existence pleasant and easy; fine dwellings, flowers, copious repasts, women luxuriously apparelled, precious fabrics, horses and dogs of fine breed. If he wished to paint a *Last Supper*, it mattered little to him that legend and history agree regarding the simplicity and the humble station of Jesus and his disciples: History and tradition did not count with him. A repast, whatever it would be, he could not conceive of, unless around a sumptuous table, covered with costly vessels, served by attendants in picturesque costumes and enlivened by the antics of buffoons or the harmonies of music. It was thus that he painted Christ, it was after this original conception that he worked out his immortal compositions. Accordingly no one could justly appraise Veronese, without first setting aside, as he did, all those historic data which he voluntarily ignored.

THE SOJOURN IN VENICE

There are few painters of whose private life so little is known as of that of Veronese. The contemporary documents have disappeared and scarcely anything more remains than a few of his letters; and even those are silent as to his day-by-day existence. All that it is possible to know – and to this his paintings abundantly bear witness – is that he was possessed of an agreeable humour, and a pleasing personality; – worthy gentleman, somewhat quick of temper and permitting no slight to be put upon his dignity, still less upon his honour. He was neither a sycophant nor a courtier, accepting commissions but never soliciting them. His "disinterestedness," writes Charles Yriarte, "has remained celebrated; during one entire period of his life, the greater part of the contracts which he signed with communities and with convents stipulate barely the value of his time as a remuneration for his work. This was before the time when painters were expected to furnish their colours and their canvases, but demanded only the price of their toil. Later on, having become, if not rich – that he never was, – at least celebrated and independent, he acquired a taste for personal luxury; he delighted in brilliant fabrics and wore them with ostentation; he loved horses, dogs, and hunting; he frequented high society, and brought to it that Italian open-heartedness which makes the company of the illustrious a relaxation and a pleasure rather than an embarrassment or an effort. He won valuable friendships and was able to retain them until his death."

Of these friendships, the most efficacious was that of the Prior of the convent of San Sebastiano, Bernardo Torlioni, a Veronese by birth, to whom he had brought letters of introduction. No sooner had young Caliari arrived in Venice at the beginning of 1555, than he presented himself to his venerable compatriot, who promptly took a fancy to him, and bestirred himself to serve him. Thanks to Torlioni, Paolo obtained an order for five pictures, including one large composition, the *Coronation of the Virgin* and four dependent panels. These paintings were destined to adorn the sacristy of the church of San Sebastiano, of which Bernardo Torlioni was prior. When the work was done, the Chapter expressed itself as so well pleased that it entrusted him with the decoration of the church itself, including the ceiling. It was here that Veronese painted his admirable series of episodes from the *History of Esther and Ahasuerus*.

The success of this series was so great that the edifice was placed unconditionally in his hands, and he was free to follow his fantasy unhampered. Following a method which was habitual with him, he enhanced the effect of the large panels painted in fresco, by means of smaller intervening scenes in chiaroscuro. Here also one finds him indulging his hobby for architectural painting, such as always occupies a large place in his pictures; all around the church he painted truncated columns, ornamented with arabesques and foliage, "with a richness and a pomp that were already an inseparable feature of his style."

In the works of Veronese, the accessories always play a highly important part; and it is not difficult to understand the reason. His main object being to delight the eye, he attributed considerable space to vases, furniture, armour, fruits, flowers, graceful draperies, brilliant costumes, mettlesome horses, and more especially dogs, with which it was his special whim to embellish his paintings. The dog was his favourite animal, and even at that epoch its presence was to be noted in every picture.

When the church, completely decorated, was opened to the public, there was general rejoicing; Veronese received the unanimous vote of approval, from the populace as well as from the artists.

From that day forth, the ability of the young painter was openly acknowledged, and his fortune assured. Furthermore, he had arrived in Venice at a propitious hour. It was the moment when the Most Serene Republic, victorious over the seas and surfeited with wealth, attained the zenith of her glory. In her opulence Venice chose to employ her treasures in self-adornment; palaces arose on all sides, the Ducal Palace itself was redecorated; Sansovino was just completing the new Government offices. The wealthy brotherhoods and equally wealthy parishes were seeking out every painter of repute to decorate their churches and their convents.

Accordingly, Veronese had arrived at the crucial moment to satisfy the demands of art. His rivals were negligible: Salviati, Battista Franco, Lo Schiavone, Zelotti, Orazio Vocelli the son of Titian, could none of them hold their own against him. Bordone was at the court of Francis I. Tintoretto alone, at the height of his powers, could counterbalance Veronese's glory. As to the aged Titian, he was no longer producing pictures with his old-time fertility; furthermore, he had already divined the genius of Veronese and conceived a friendship for him.

And so, throughout thirty-three years, from 1555 to 1588, the masterpieces that were born beneath Veronese's fingers succeeded one another without interruption. The walls of his adopted city became overspread with his luminous canvases, eloquent of the joyousness of Italy, resplendent with the triumphant beauty of Venice.

Shortly after the decoration of San Sebastiano was completed, Daniele Barbaro, Patriarch of Aquileia and wealthy patrician of Venice, had a splendid residence built him at Masiera by Palladio, a celebrated architect of the period. Being a man of artistic taste, he wished to embellish it with paintings and statues worthy of its imposing architecture. For the sculpture he summoned Alessandro Vittoria; the paintings were entrusted to Paolo Veronese.

The patriarch Barbaro was one of his friends, and accordingly allowed him a free hand, and even left the choice of subjects to him.

Veronese, who was a prodigiously fertile artist, left not a single space in Barbaro's house unoccupied with colour. Wherever space would not permit of large compositions, he painted trophies, garlands, flowers, even statues, possessing all the lustre and relief of marble. Elsewhere he sketched in architectural fantasies, simulating colonnades and porticoes, opening upon landscapes borrowed from the realm of dreams; he conceived imaginary doors, before which fictitious lacqueys appeared to be standing. The principal subjects treated by Veronese at Masiera include *Nobility*, *Honour*, *Magnificence*, *Vice*, *Virtue*, *Flora*, *Pomona*, *Ceres* and *Bacchus*; then in the ceiling of the cupola he gathered together all the gods of Olympus, grouped around Jupiter.

The decorations in the palace at Masiera further augmented Veronese's fame. He was now acknowledged to be the foremost painter of Venice, next to Titian. Barbaro had been so delighted with his talents that he determined to do him a service. Standing well at court, he recommended him to the Signoria. As a result of this, the latter entrusted him with the task of redecorating the halls and chambers of the Doge's Palace, in conjunction with Tintoretto and Orazio Titian. Which of the three artists proved superior it is impossible to decide to-day, because a fire, occurring in 1576, destroyed their paintings along with the palace. But public opinion of that period gave the palm to Veronese.

It seems as though this verdict must have been justified, in view of the esteem in which his name was held.

Shortly afterwards, Sansovino having completed the construction of the library, the procurators instructed the architect to arrange with Titian as to a choice of painters to decorate it in competition. Veronese was immediately designated, together with

Zelotti, Batista Franco, Giuseppe Salviati, Lo Schiavene and Il Fratina, who were to divide the twenty-one ceiling panels between them. Three round compartments fell to the lot of Veronese, who filled them with figures representing *Music, Geometry with Arithmetic*, and *Honour*. Under Veronese's brush these cold abstractions took on the most charming forms; they were represented by graceful women, each surrounded by the attributes of the science which she symbolized. A recompense was promised by the procurators to the artist whose paintings should be adjudged most beautiful. Titian was enthusiastic over those of Veronese. Loyal and noble artist that he was, he himself solicited the votes of the painters who had taken part in the competition, and thus Veronese was declared winner by the voice of his own competitors. The senate offered him a golden chain which he delighted to wear on solemn occasions.

These great official works did not diminish the number of his productions for churches, convents, or private persons of wealth. No other artist affords an example of similar fecundity.

And what verges upon prodigy is that he never employed collaborators, as so many other celebrated painters have done; the only one that he is known to have had is his brother Benedetto Caliari, whose artistic aid was limited to painting in the prospective of the vast architectural designs with which it pleased Veronese to embellish all his canvases.

The epoch of his most fertile production was between 1562 and 1565; it was also the period in which he executed his largest and most celebrated paintings, notably his famous canvas of the *Wedding at Cana*, his *Feast at the House of the Pharisee*, his *Feast at the House of the Leper*, and his *Feast at the House of Simon*.

These four pictures are known under the name of the four *Feasts*. Two of them belong to France and hang in the museum of the Louvre, in the room known by the name of the *Salon Carré*; these are the *Feast at the House of Simon the Pharisee* and the *Wedding at Cana*.

THE WEDDING AT CANA

Veronese has treated this subject twice. Accordingly the picture in the Louvre must not be confounded with that of the same name in the Brera museum at Milan. In spite of the value of the latter, it bears no comparison to the gigantic canvas in the national museum of France.

This picture of the *Wedding at Cana* was painted by Veronese for the refectory of the convent of San Giorgio Maggiore, on the island that faces the *Riva dei Schiavoni*. It remained there until the time of Napoleon's Italian Campaign. Bonaparte, who loved the arts without understanding them, laid profane hands on the great majority of Italian masterpieces. This painting by Veronese was one of the number, and found a place in the Louvre. The treaty of 1815 obliged France to restore these treasures, but the Austrian commissioners, appointed to accomplish the restitution, became alarmed at the difficulties of transportation which the *Wedding at Cana* presented. They accordingly consented to exchange this canvas for a painting by Le Brun, *The Feast at the House of the Pharisee*. Veronese's masterpiece remained in the Louvre, in which it is one of the most flawless gems.

The contract drawn up between Veronese and the Prior of San Giorgio Maggiore for the execution of this picture has been preserved. The painter bound himself to deliver it within a year, since the contract was signed June 6, 1562 and the delivery of the canvas took place of September 8, 1563. He was to be furnished with canvas and colours, to be entitled to take his meals at the convent and receive a cask of wine as additional recompense. As to remuneration for his work, it was fixed by mutual agreement at 324 ducats, which, in the 16th century, corresponded to 972 francs in the coin of France. Taking into consideration the enhanced value of money since that epoch, these 972 francs would represent to-day 7,000 francs. Such is the price which the greatest artist of his time received for a masterpiece which to-day commands the admiration of the entire world.

Never did Veronese display so much brilliance, dispense so much imagination as in the *Wedding at Cana*; never did he show a greater dexterity in execution; for, however considerable the dimensions of the canvas may be, it demanded nothing less than genius to distribute without clash or disproportion the hundred and thirty-two personages which compose it. A painter less thoroughly sure of himself would have made a sorry mess of this Feast; Veronese has produced a composition that is admirable for its balance, in abounding charming details, and unexpected and picturesque episodes, that do not in the least detract from the effect of the painting as a whole.

On this picture, as on so many others from the brush of Veronese, one cannot, as has already been said, pass an equitable judgment, unless one accepts, without question, the master's method. Veronese had no more respect for religious tradition than he had for mythological legend. To take issue with the incongruities and anachronisms of the *Wedding at Cana*, is voluntarily to debar oneself from discussing it. If historic exactitude is the one thing that counts in a painting, then this picture simply does not exist. But happily painting has no need to justify itself to history; it is amply sufficient to itself, without borrowing anything from history, and loses nothing of its beauty if perchance it does violence to history. And of this the *Wedding at Cana* furnishes a most eloquent proof.

The composition of this famous picture is well known. Jesus is seated in the middle focus, at the centre of the table, which is curved on each side in the form of a horse-shoe. To fill this immense table, Veronese did not go to the scriptures in search of personages; he drew them from his surroundings and from his own imagination.

The groom, a handsome, black bearded young man, clad in purple and gold, is no other than Alphonso d'Avalos, Marquis del Vasto, and the bride is a portrait of Eleanora of Austria, sister of Charles V., and Queen of France. On the left, one discovers, with some surprise, Francis I., Charles V., the Sultan Achmed II., and Queen Mary of England. Beside the Sultan is a woman richly robed and holding a tooth-pick; she is Vittoria Colonna, Marchesa di Pescara; then, further on are monks, cardinals, and personal friends of the artist. Standing up, clad in brocade and holding a cup in his hand, is Veronese's brother, Benedetto Caliari. In the centre are a group of musicians. The octogenarian bending over his viol, is a portrait of Titian; Bassano is playing the flute; Tintoretto and Veronese himself draw their bow across the strings of a 'cello.

The success of the *Wedding at Cana* was triumphal. The great painters of Venice, contemporaries of Veronese, overwhelmed him with proofs of their admiration; even morose Tintoretto found some extremely amiable words in which to praise his rival in fame, and Titian embraced the happy painter when he chanced to meet him in the city streets.

These praises were merited; the *Wedding at Cana* is quite truly one of the most beautiful masterpieces in the world's collection of paintings.

The renown obtained by this admirable work brought Veronese a host of orders. The various cities vied with each other to secure him to decorate their churches or their convents. His first patron, the Prior Torlioni, ordered a picture from him for the convent of San Sebastiano, the church of which he had already decorated. Veronese, by no means ungrateful, painted for him the *Feast at the House of the Leper*, in 1570; three years later he painted for the dominican monastery of San Giovanni e Paolo the *Feast at the House of Levi*, to decorate one side of the refectory. The monks had only a modest sum at their disposal and tremblingly offered it to the now celebrated painter; they naïvely added the donation of a few casks of wine. Veronese exhibited the most complete disinterestedness by accepting these humble offers of the Prior. This was his third *Feast*.

The fourth, known under the name of the *Feast at the House of Simon the Pharisee*, was executed for the refectory of the Brotherhood of Servites. It represents Magdalen on her knees, wiping the feet of Christ with her hair. This painting now hangs in the Louvre, opposite the *Wedding at Cana*. It has been the property of France for two centuries, and the history of its acquisition by Louis XIV is curious enough to be worth the telling. Colbert, having learned that Spain had negotiated for the purchase of the *Feast at the House of Simon*, resolved to go to any lengths in order to acquire it himself, on behalf of Louis XIV. The French ambassador to Venice, Pierre de Bonzi, was charged with the negotiations. To address himself directly to the Servites was impossible, since there was a law in the Venetian Republic forbidding the sale and exportation of any native works of art. Bonzi pursued the course of informing the Signoria of his royal master's wish. The Signoria, desirous of securing the good will of the great king, without violating her own laws, purchased with public funds the picture from the Servites, and straight way offered it to Louis XIV, who returned warm thanks to his "very dear and great friends, allies and confederates, after having seen this rare and most perfect original."

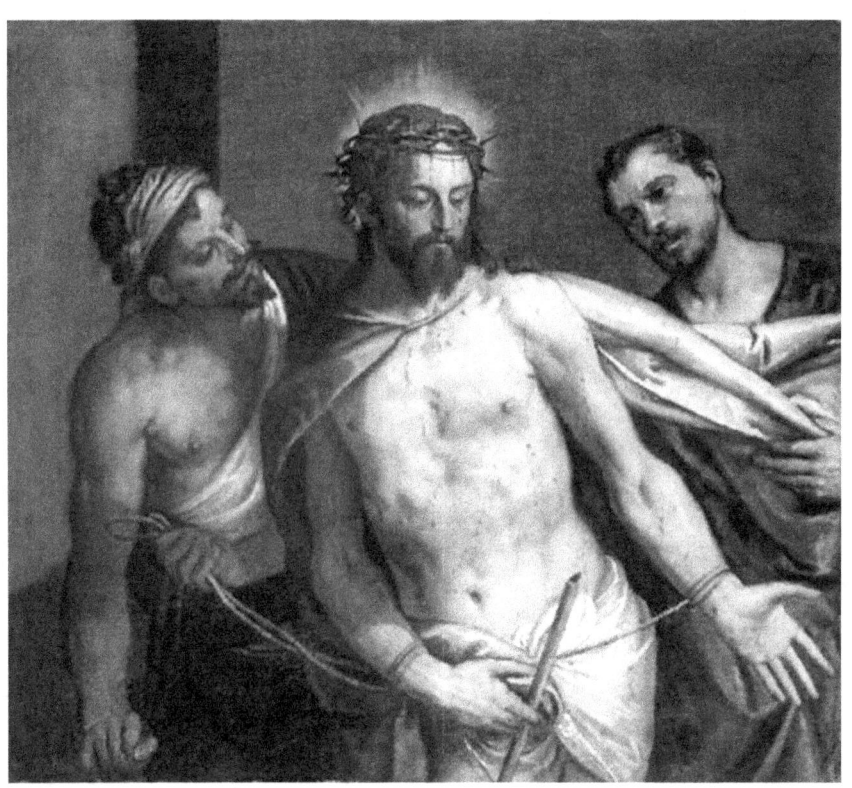

Paolo Veronese, Ecce Homo

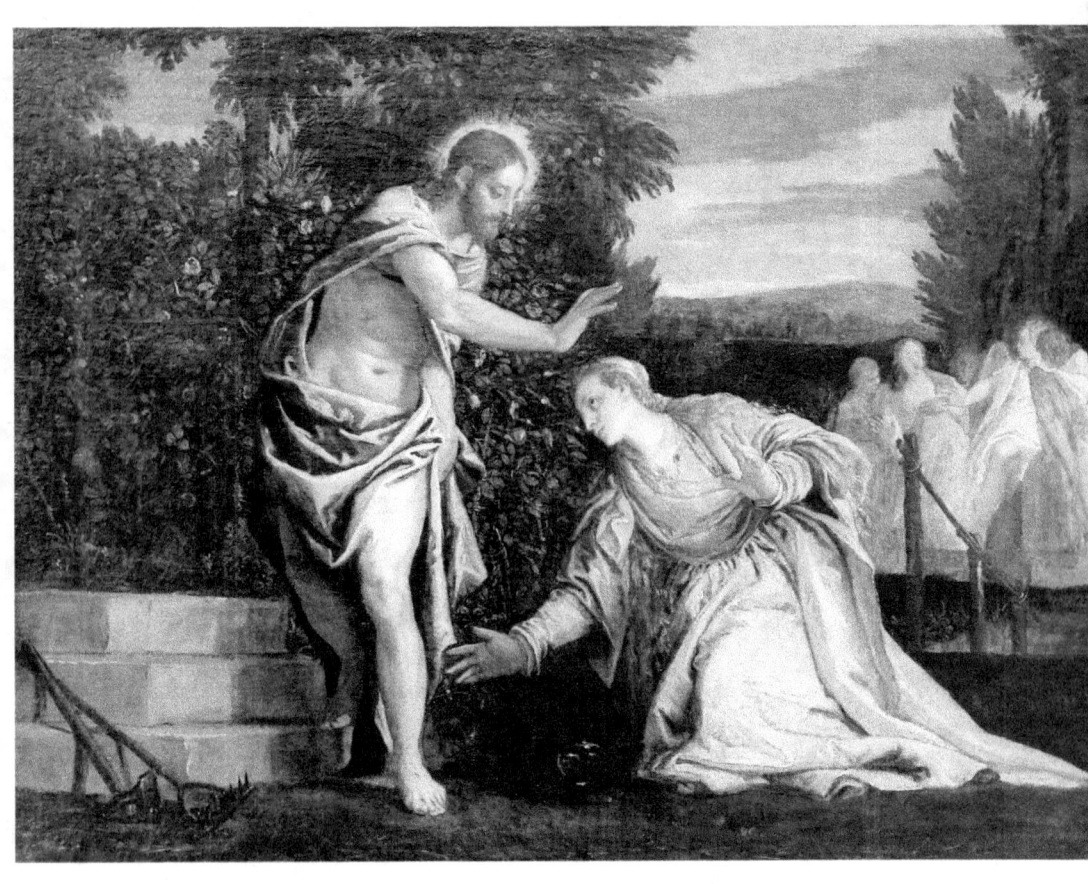

Paolo Veronese, Noli Me Tangere

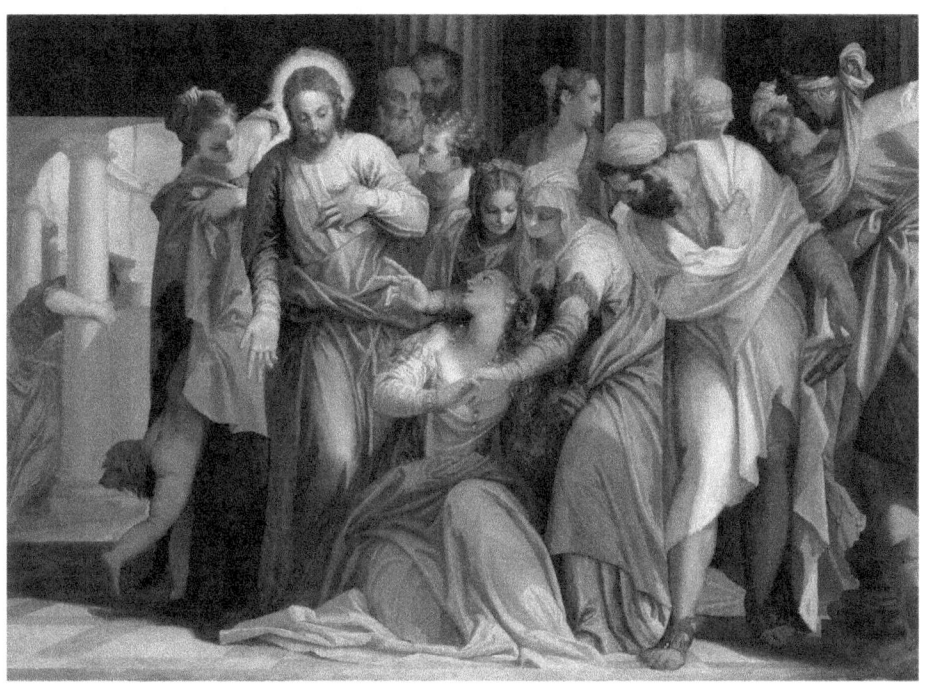

Paolo Veronese, The Conversion of Mary Magdalene, 1548

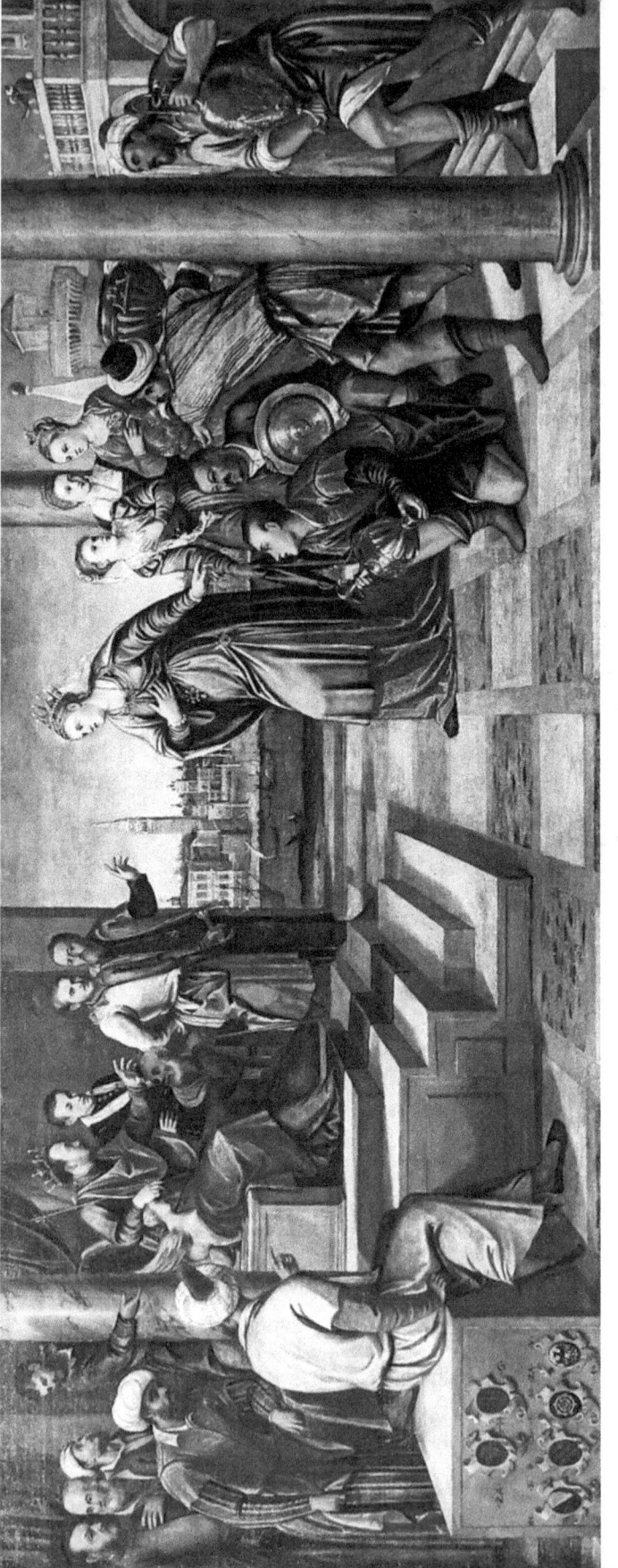

Paolo Veronese, Sacristy, Visit of the Queen of Sheba To Solomon, Venice

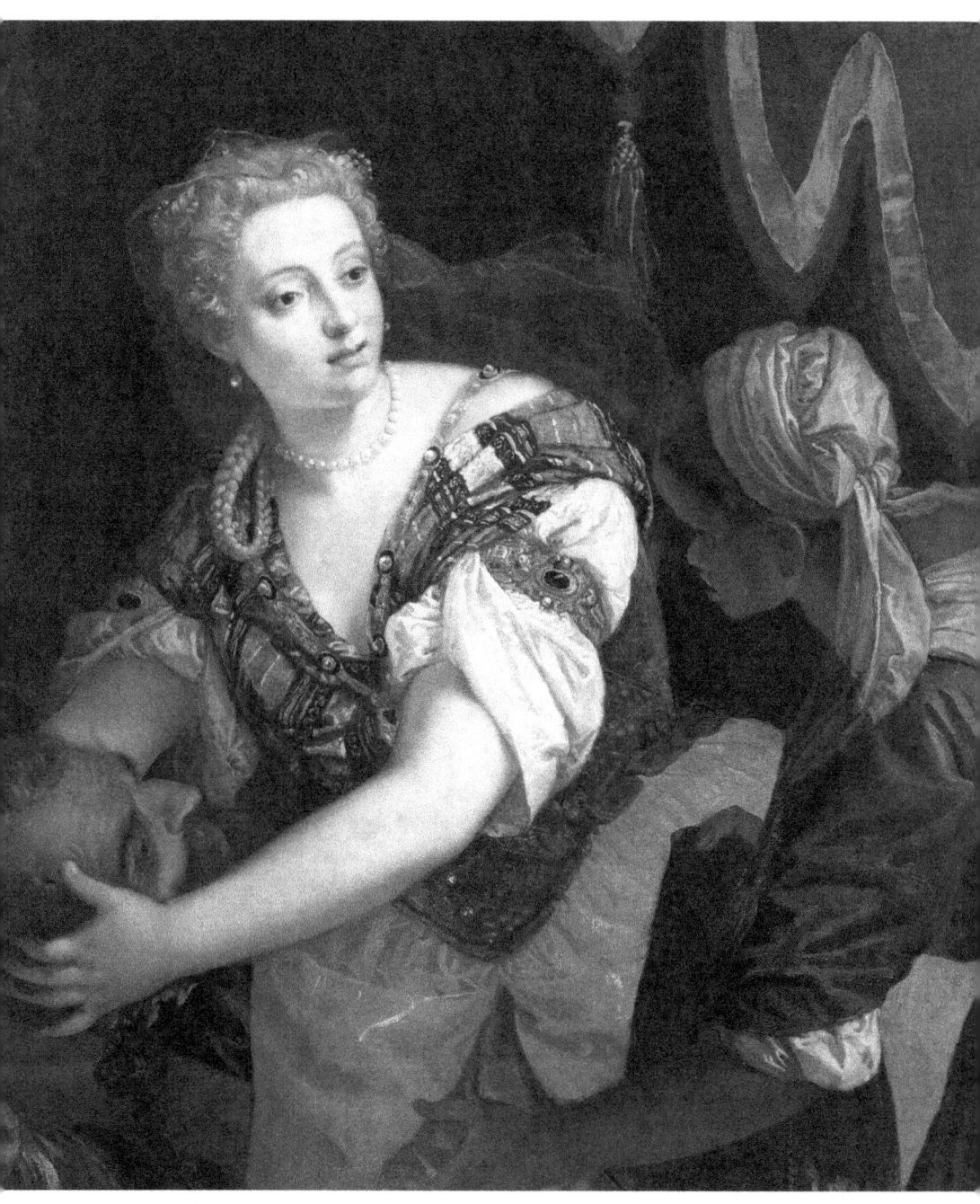

Paolo Veronese, Judith With the Head of Holofernes, 1575-80

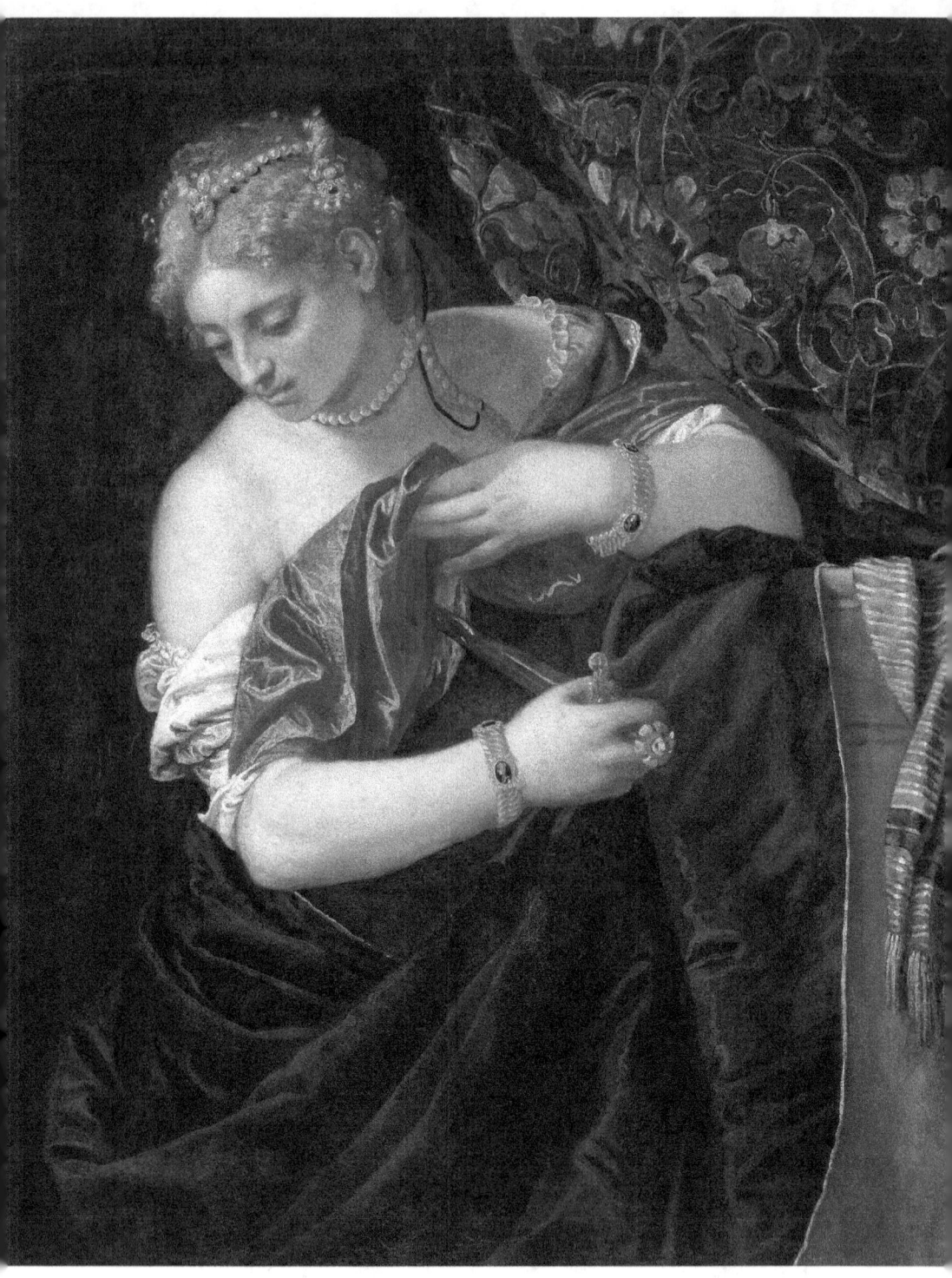

Paolo Veronese, Lucrezia, 1561, Vienna

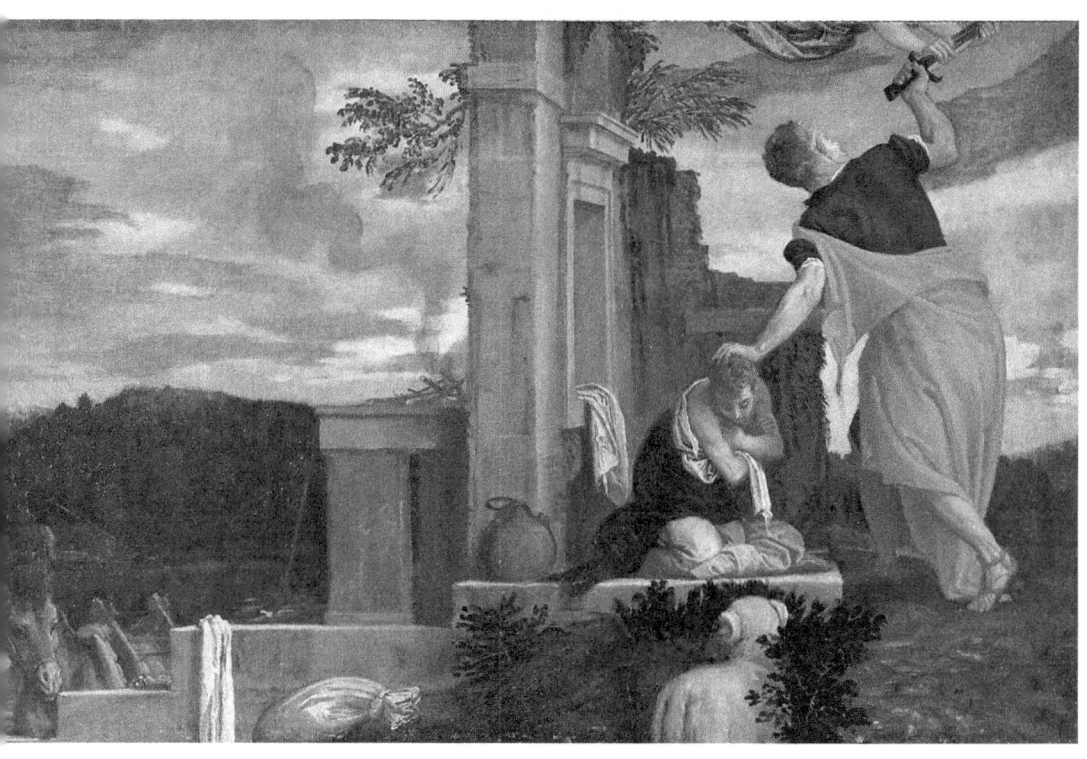

Paolo Veronese, The Binding of Isaac, 1588, Kunsthistorisches Museum

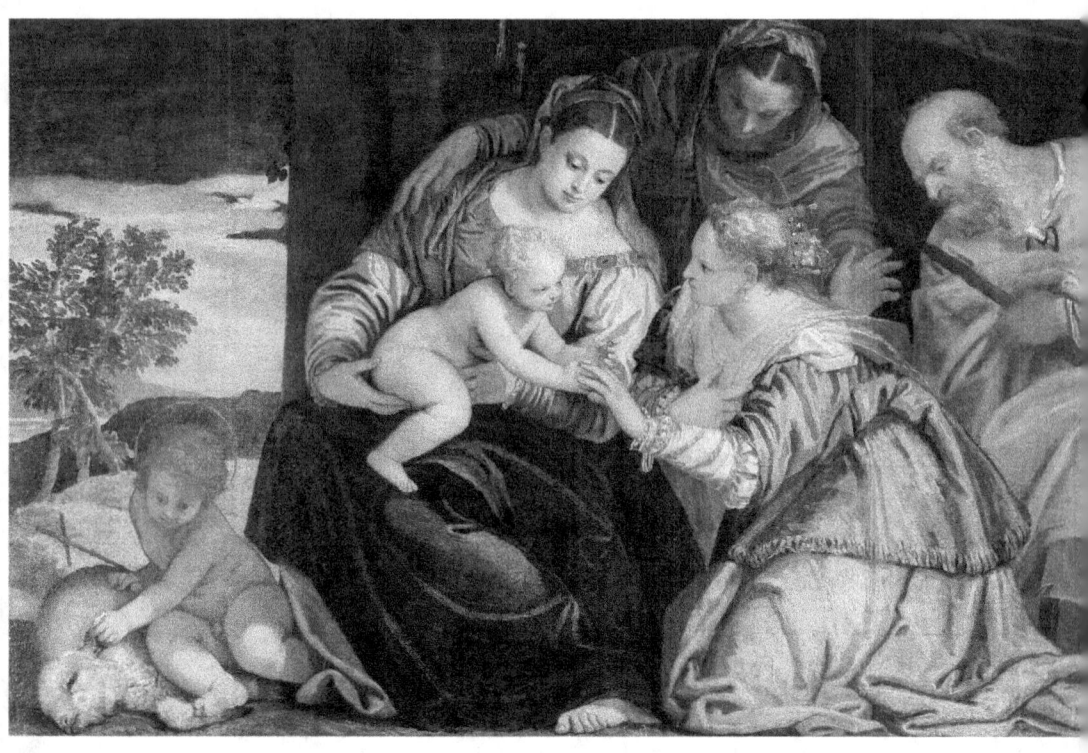

Paolo Veronese, The Mystic Marriage of St Catherine, 1555

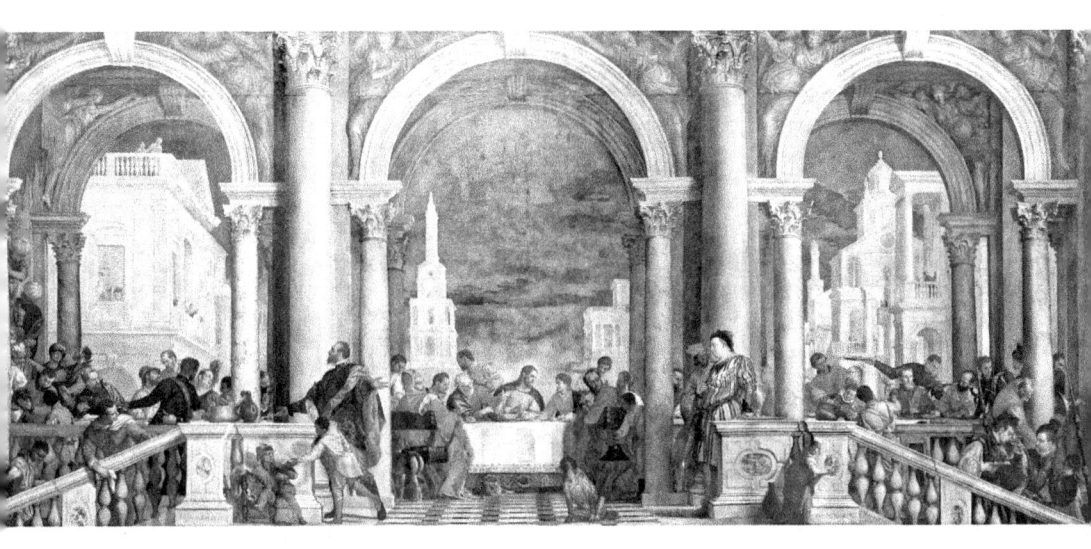

Paolo Veronese, The Feast In the House of Levi, 1573

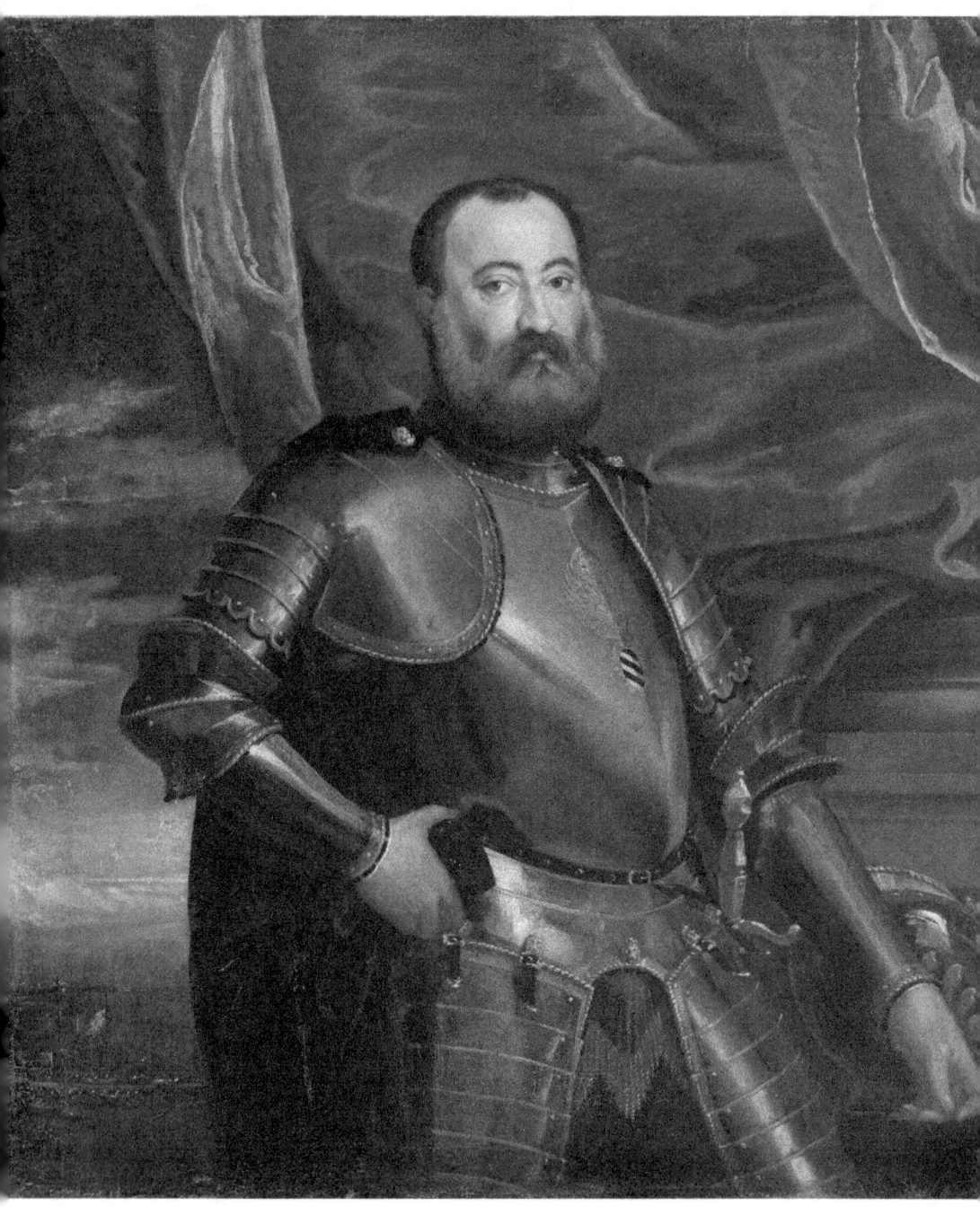

Paolo Veronese, Portrait of Girolamo Contarini, 1570

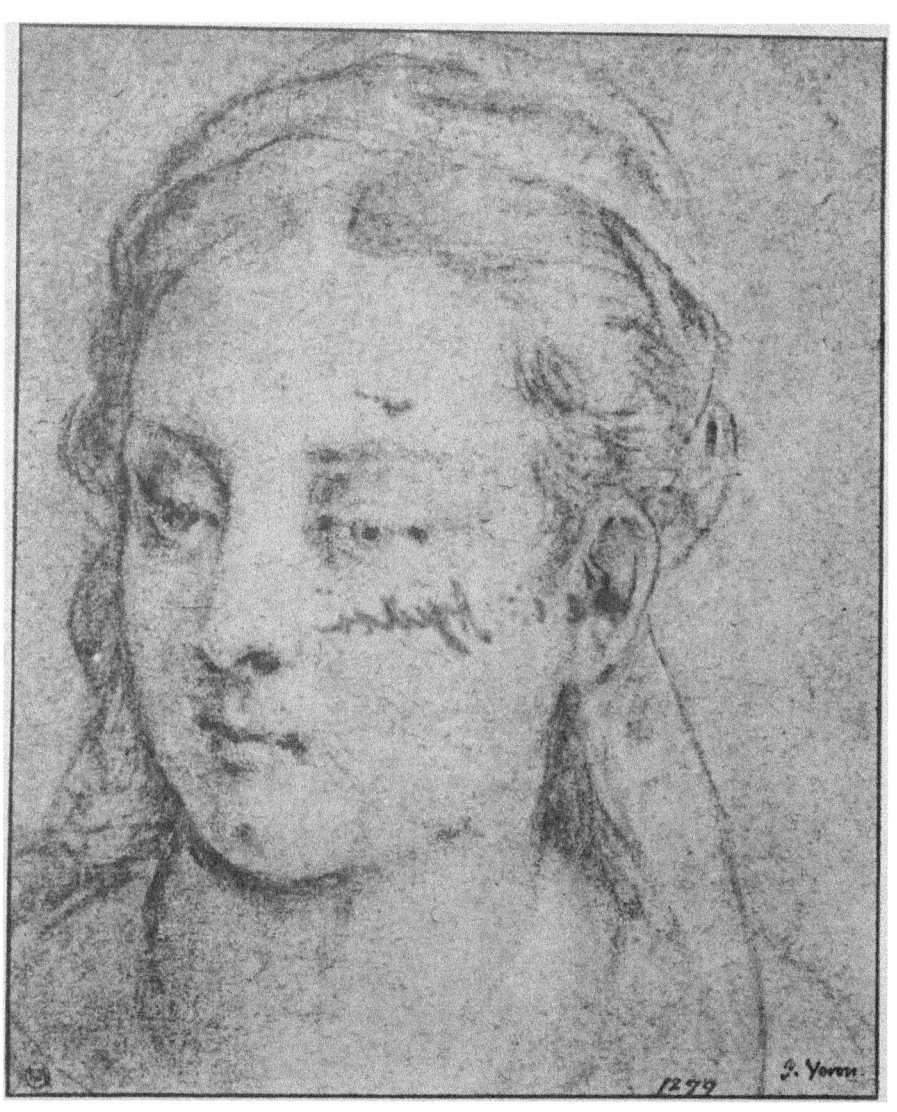

Paolo Veronese, Drawing

VERONESE AND
THE INQUISITION

These four *Feasts* of Veronese won him a widespread renown. But there were certain hostile spirits, uncompromising traditionalists, to whom the fantastic elements which he introduced into the composition of his religious pictures were necessarily strongly displeasing. To introduce dwarfs, buffoons, men at arms under the influence of liquor, at a feast where Jesus and his disciples take part, – did not this savour of irreverence, nay, worse than that, of heresy?

The *Feast at the House of Levi the Publican*, executed for the convent of San Giovanni e Paolo, in which Veronese had given free rein to his imagination, was denounced to the Holy Office, and on July 18, 1573, the artist was summoned before the tribunal of the Inquisition.

In the Most Serene Republic this tribunal scarcely had the same redoubtable power with which the sombre fanaticism of Philip II had armed it in Spain. It was none the less a grave risk to incur its displeasure at an epoch when the Papacy still held undisputed sway over the guidance of souls. Consequently this prosecution caused Veronese serious alarm.

M. Armand Baschet discovered quite recently in the archives of the Frari, at Venice, the official record of the trial with all the questions put to him and his answers.

＊ 42

The judges took special exception to his *Feast at the House of Levi*, which seemed to them an outrage upon religion. Each one of the figures in the picture was brought up separately for discussion, and the luckless Veronese was required to make explanation. What was the significance of that man who was bleeding at the nose? Why were those two soldiers, on the steps of the stairway, one of them drinking and the other eating, clad in German uniform? And, at a repast where the Saviour figures, what was that ridiculous buffoon doing with a parroquet on his wrist?

Veronese defended himself as best he could. He assumed a sort of injured innocence and apparently failed to understand the enormity of the irreverence with which he was charged. Next, he took shelter behind the precedent established by the great masters. He cited Michelangelo and his *Last Judgment*:

"At Rome, in the Pope's own chapel, Michelangelo has represented Our Lord, his Mother, Saint John, Saint Peter and the Celestial Choir, and he has represented them all naked, even the Virgin Mary, and that, too, in diverse attitudes, such as were certainly not inspired by our greatest of religions."

Finally, Veronese emphatically denied the charge of any intentional irreverence toward the Church; he declared that he had simply permitted himself, perhaps wrongfully, a certain amount of license such as is accorded to poets and to fools.

His contrite attitude won him the indulgence of the Tribunal. But the judges demanded that he should correct his picture, and he was obliged to remove the dwarfs and the fools and to modify the attitude of his men at arms. This is the picture that may be seen to-day at the Accademia delle Belle Arti, at Venice, retouched in accordance with the orders of the Holy Office.

THE JOURNEY TO ROME

In spite of his keen desire to pay a visit to Rome, Veronese was kept in Venice by his ceaseless productivity, and he attained the age of forty without ever having had the chance of a sight of the Eternal City. Of all the masterpieces in that home of the Pontiffs, he knew nothing, excepting of such as he had seen copied in the form of engravings. The appointment of his friend and patron as ambassador to the Holy See, afforded him an opportunity to make the journey so many times projected and deferred.

No documents exist regarding Veronese's sojourn in Rome, but at all events it was fairly brief. Beyond this, we are reduced to mere conjecture. Furthermore, there is no extant evidence to sustain the idea that he practised his art in the Eternal City. If he had painted any pictures there, some trace of them would surely have been discovered. It must therefore be concluded that he contented himself with admiring the masterpieces with which his illustrious predecessors, Raphael and Michelangelo, had enriched the capital of the Pontiffs.

But his temperament was too peculiar, his manner too individual, and we may as well acknowledge, his nature too superficial, to permit of his experiencing those profound and overwhelming impressions that radically modify an artistic career.

And for this we ought rather to be thankful than to complain, since it was only his obstinate insistence upon remaining himself that saved Veronese from shipwreck upon the ever threatening reef of imitation.

THE RETURN TO VENICE

From the moment of his return to Venice, Veronese was besieged from all sides; once again he found himself enslaved to forced labor by the incessant contracts demanded of him by his fellow citizens. The scantiness of documents which we possess regarding his life does not permit us to name the chronological order in which he painted his pictures. We shall therefore gather them into groups for the sake of convenience in studying his more important works. Furthermore, to study one by one, all of his paintings, is not to be thought of; for this painter was one of the most prolific producers of which the history of art makes mention. In every one of his pictures will be found, more or less accentuated, those qualities of composition, of picturesqueness, and of colour which together constitute his glory. Accordingly we shall limit ourselves to indicating, at the different stages of his career, those pictures which show most deeply the imprint of his genius and which also are most closely related to the life of Venice of which he was, in a certain way, together with Tintoretto, the official painter. For the rest the reader may be referred to the complete catalogue of the works of Veronese given at the close of this book.

Concerning the private life of the artist we are as poorly informed as concerning the date of his pictures. We know only that he married and that he had two sons, Gabriele and Carletto.

When they were old enough to hold a brush he entrusted them to Bassano, a Venetian painter whose talent he held in high esteem. As regards himself, the documents of the period vaunt his uprightness, his honesty and his keen sense of honour. Ridolfi, one of his biographers, who wrote sixty years after Veronese's death, and relied upon the recollections of people who knew him personally, pictured him as a man of strict principles and settled habits, and economical almost to the point of avarice. He cites, as an example of this, that the artist rarely employed ultramarine, which was very costly at that time, and thus condemned his works to premature deterioration.

His fortune, the extent of which we learn from the fiscal records of Venice, consisted in a few holdings of real estate at Castelfranco in Trevisano. In 1585 he purchased a small estate at Santa Maria in Porto, not far from the Pineta of Ravenna. He also possessed a bank account representing approximately six thousand sequins. But what was that for a man who was the most famous and the most fertile artist of his time?

We have already given examples of his disinterestedness. Many a time he refused opportunities of great wealth. He even declined the offers made him by Philip II, who tried to lure him to Spain and would have entrusted him with decorating the Escurial.

It was about the period of his return to Venice that Veronese completed his celebrated picture: *The Family of Darius at the Feet of Alexander after the Battle of Issus*, now in the National Gallery at London. The episode is well known; Darius III., King of Persia, conquered at Issus by Alexander, sends his wife and children to beg for clemency from the victor. Admitted to the conqueror's tent, the unfortunate wife perceives a warrior in resplendent garments whom she takes for Alexander, and throws herself at his feet. The warrior, however, is only Ephestion, Alexander's lieutenant and friend. The wife of Darius apologizes for her mistake, but Alexander raises her up and says: "You made no mistake, he also is Alexander."

Such is the historic theme. But what matters history to

Veronese? Upon this classic subject he has built the most fantastic, the most improbable, and at the same time the most fascinating of his compositions. The picture was painted for the Pisani family which had given him hospitality, and every one of the figures contained in it represents a member of that household.

It is related that, in order to spare his hosts the necessity of thanking him or the obligation of making some return, he rolled up his canvas and slipped it behind his bed in such a way that it would not be discovered in his room until after his departure.

It is scarcely probable that Veronese could have painted so large a canvas – fourteen metres by seven – in the necessarily brief space of a friendly visit, or that he could have painted in his figures, which are all of them portraits, without the knowledge of the Pisani family. But the anecdote is so pretty that it is pleasant to accept it as true.

It was a direct descendant of the Venetian Procurator, Count Victor Pisani, who sold the painting to England in 1857.

THE DECORATION OF THE DUCAL PALACE

In 1577 a violent conflagration destroyed the greater part of the Ducal Palace. In this disaster all the pictures perished with which Tintoretto, Horatio the son of Titian, and Veronese, had decorated it.

Desiring to restore the palace promptly and give it a new splendour, the Senate appointed a committee, authorized to distribute orders among the painters and decorators of Venice. The competitors were numerous and eager to secure a chance to collaborate in so glorious an enterprise; and to this end they paid eager court to the committee. Veronese alone made no advances, being unwilling to appear solicitous. This dignified course was looked upon as excess of pride, and one day when Jacopo Contanari met him in the street he reproached him with it. Veronese replied that it was not his business to seek for honours but to be deserving of them, and that he had less skill in soliciting work than in executing it.

But they could not exclude Veronese, whose fame had now become universal. Accordingly he was chosen with Tintoretto, and to them were added Francisco Bassano and the younger Palma. The Ducal Palace is therefore a sort of museum of the works of these masters, and forms the most brilliant collection of paintings relating to the public life and the glorification of Venice.

Veronese was entrusted with the decoration of the great central oval of the ceiling, and the lateral panels. In these he painted the *Defence of Scutari*, the *Taking of Smyrna*, and the *Triumph of Venice*. This last named painting is considered by many as Veronese's crowning achievement.

Venice is here represented in the form of a superb and smiling woman, seated upon the clouds, her eyes raised towards Glory, who offers her a crown. At her side, Renown celebrates her grandeur; at her feet are grouped Honour, Liberty, Peace, Juno, and Ceres; lower down an ethereal structure of admirable daring and architectural beauty sustains a great assemblage of gentlemen and ladies richly clad, of cardinals and bishops, all emulously uniting in the glorification of Venice. On the ground level standards, trophies, and cavaliers add the finishing touch to the composition, and are treated with incomparable vigour and skill both in chiaroscuro and in perspective.

Although of more modest dimensions, the *Taking of Smyrna* and the *Defence of Scutari* are in no wise inferior to the great central composition. In this same Hall of the Grand Council, Veronese painted two other great canvases, representing the Military Expedition of the Doges, Loredan and Mocenigo.

But for that matter there is not a room in the Palace of the Doges in which Veronese is not represented by one or more canvases; in the Hall of the Anticollegio, there is a ceiling painting representing *Venice Enthroned*, a work that has unfortunately deteriorated; in the Hall of the Collegio, a *Battle of Lepanto*, a *Christ in Glory, Venice and the Doge Venier*, a *Faith*, a *St. Mark*, and a ceiling which is considered as the most beautiful in the whole Palace of the Doges: *Venice Upon the Terrestrial Globe, Between Justice and Peace*. The Hall of the Council of Ten contains, in the oval ceiling panel: *An Old Man resting his Head on his Hand* and *A Young Woman*. In the Hall of the "Bussola," *St. Mark crowning the Theological Virtues*, the original of which is at the present time in the Louvre. Mention should also be made of: The

Triumph of the Doge Venier over the Turks; the *Return of Contanari, Victor over the Genoese at Chioggia*; the *Emperor Frederick at the feet of Alexander III.*, and, in the Hall of the Ambassadors, a magnificent allegory of Venice, personified as a patrician lady seen from behind, robed in white satin and of marvellous grace.

Veronese also had a share in the decoration of another of Venice's monumental buildings, situated near the bridge of the Rialto and known by the name of the Fondaco dei Tedeschi. This building, which is to-day occupied by the Post Office, formerly served as warehouse for German business men having commercial relations with the Republic. These rich merchants had had the palace adorned by the greatest painters in Venice. Giorgione and Titian had decorated its walls not only within, but also on the exterior, where traces of the paintings can still be seen. Veronese was entrusted with four compositions, one of which is an allegory representing *Germany receiving the Imperial Crown*. It is believed that the canvas now in the Museum at Berlin, entitled *Jupiter, Fortune and Germany*, once formed part of the decoration of the Fondaco dei Tedeschi. It was purchased at Verona in 1841. Veronese's celebrity, about the year 1580, had become world-wide. Every sovereign who prided himself on his art gallery wished to possess some of his work. The indefatigable artist endeavoured to satisfy them all; he even corresponded personally with several of them. For the Duke of Savoy, he painted *The Queen of Sheba Visiting Solomon*; to the Duke of Mantua, who had honoured him with his friendship, he sent a *Moses Saved from the Waters*; to the Emperor Rudolph II. he gave a *Cephale and Procris* and a *Poem of Venus*. These last two canvases, of which the German Emperor was very proud, were taken from him by Gustavus Adolphus, when that triumphant conqueror passed through Vienna.

Throughout his life, Veronese remained faithful to the pompous, brilliant, ornamental school of painting. Not that he was incapable of essaying other types, but because it was his own preference to paint ease and luxury on a broad scale. He sometimes had occasion to handle more vigorous subjects, and in this he was completely successful, as the magnificent painting entitled *Jupiter Destroying the Vices* abundantly bears witness.

The surprise experienced in the presence of this noble work, executed with the energy of a master-hand, is surpassed only by admiration for the versatility of a genius which could at will adapt itself to unfamiliar formulas. This famous painting, proud and virile in style, was taken from Italy by the victorious Armies of France, and placed in Versailles in the chamber of Louis XIV., where for a long period it served as the ceiling decoration. It was finally removed and now hangs in the Louvre, in company of other masterpieces by the same artist.

THE LAST YEARS

The execution of his large official canvases did not prevent Veronese from responding to all the appeals which came to him from every side. His unequalled activity, his prodigious facility made it possible for him to satisfy these demands. No one knows all the pictures which he painted for private individuals, nor all the frescoes with which he adorned certain dwellings that have since disappeared. Nevertheless what a formidable list the works of this painter would make if the attempt were made to draw up such a list without omissions! Ridolfi devotes not less than thirty pages to a simple enumeration of the pictures which Veronese painted for the neighbouring islands of Venice, such as Murano and Torcello, for the country house of the Grimani at Orlago, for that of the Duke of Tuscany at Artemino, or for the Palace of the Pisani. To Verona, to Brescia, to Vicenza, to Treviso, to Padua; to Venice also, to the Frari, to Ognissanti, to the Umilta, to San Francisco del Orto, to Santa Catarina, for which he painted his famous *Marriage of St. Catherine*, everywhere, in short, where they required him, he sent marvellous canvases, magic with colour and with life; – canvases for which to-day museums vie with each other for their weight in gold.

But Veronese was no longer young; he had entered well into the fifties; yet nothing in his craftsmanship betrayed fatigue or waning powers. A genius almost unique, he went steadily forward and no one could say of him, in the presence of his latest productions, what has so often been said of other illustrious painters: "That is a work of his old age!" Veronese had the rare privilege of remaining young to the end.

One day, while following a procession on foot, Veronese contracted a cold, and after a brief illness he died. His obsequies took place in the parish church of San Samuele, April 19, 1588. On that day he would have completed his sixtieth year.

When we remember that, up to the eve of his death, Veronese continued to paint with as steady a hand as at the age of twenty, his death seems premature, and it is only natural to deplore that this matchless artist should have failed to obtain the ripe age of Titian. What masterpieces he might still have painted!

Such as they are, brilliant and luxuriant, his works remain the most abundant that have ever come from the palette of any one painter, and Veronese stands lastingly, in the history of Art, as the most amazing of all masters, both in colour and in composition.

THE WORKS OF
PAOLO VERONESE

FRANCE

PARIS (MUSEUM OF THE LOUVRE): The Wedding at Cana. – The Feast at the House of Simon the Pharisee. – Jupiter destroying the Vices. – Portrait of a Young Woman. – Susannah and the Elders. – The Disciples at Emmaüs. – The Fainting of Esther. – The Burning of Sodom. – Two Holy Families. – Calvary. – Jesus Stumbling Beneath the Weight of the Cross. – St. Mark Crowning the Theological Virtues. – Jesus Curing Peter's Mother-in-law.

MONTPELLIER (MUSEUM): The Virgin in the Clouds. – The Marriage of St. Catherine. – St. Francis Receiving the Stigmata.

RENNES (MUSEUM): Perseus Delivering Andromeda.

LILLE (MUSEUM): Science and Eloquence. – The Martyrdom of St. George.

ROUEN (MUSEUM): St. Barnabas Curing the Sick.

ENGLAND

LONDON (NATIONAL GALLERY): The Rape of Europa. –
The Family of Darius. – Magdalen at the Feet of the Saviour. –
The Vision of St. Helena. – The Adoration of the Magi. – The
Consecration of St. Nicholas.

EDINBURGH (NATIONAL GALLERY): Venus and Adonis. –
Mars and Venus.

DULWICH COLLEGE: A Cardinal pronouncing Benediction.

ITALY

VENICE (ACCADEMIA DELLE BELLE ARTI): St. Mark and
St. Matthew. – The Feast at the House of Levi – St. Luke and St.
John. – St. Christina fed by the Angels. – St. Christina thrown into
the Lake of Bolsena. – The Virgin, St. Joseph and several Saints. –
The Virgin and St. Dominique. – St. Christina before the False
Gods. – The Annunciation. – The Coronation of the Virgin. –
Isaiah. – Ezechiel. – The Battle of Cursolari. – The Flagellation of
St. Christina. – The Angels of the Passion. – Jesus and the two
Thieves.

VENICE (DUCAL PALACE): The Triumph of Venice. – The
Rape of Europa. – Peace and Justice.

ASOLO (VILLA BARBARO): Fresco Decorations.

ROME (VATICAN): St. Helena.

FLORENCE (UFFIZZI GALLERY): Esther before Ahasuerus.
– Portrait of a Man. – Jesus Crucified. – Prudence, Hope, and
Love. – The Annunciation to the Virgin. – The Martyrdom of St.

Justine. – The Martyrdom of St. Catherine. – The Madonna and the Infant Jesus (Sketch). – Study for a St. Paul. – Gentleman in a white Robe (Sketch). – Holy Family with St. Catherine.

FLORENCE (PITTI PALACE): Portrait of Veronese's Wife. – Portrait of Daniele Barbaro. – The Baptism of Christ. – Portrait of a Child. – Christ taking leave of His Mother.

BERGAMO (CARRARA ACADEMY): Reunion in a Garden. – Episode from the Life of St. Catherine.

TURIN (ROYAL MUSEUM): Magdalen washing the Feet of Christ. – Moses saved from the Waters.

NAPLES (NATIONAL MUSEUM): The Circumcision.

GENOA (DORIA PALACE): Susannah and the Elders. – The same Subject. – Allegorical Figures.

MODENA (ROYAL GALLERY OF ESTE): St. Peter and St. Paul. – Portrait of Veronese. – A Captain.

MILAN (BRERA MUSEUM): The Feast at the House of the Pharisee. – The Adoration of the Magi. – The Last Supper. – The Baptism of Christ. – St. Gregory and St. Jerome Glorified. – St. Ambrose and St. Augustine Glorified. – Christ on the Mount of Olives. – St. Anthony, St. Cornelius and St. Cyprian.

BELGIUM

BRUSSELS (ROYAL MUSEUM): The Adoration of the Magi. – The Holy Family with St. Theresa and St. Catherine. – Juno lavishing her Treasures on Venice.

SPAIN

MADRID (MUSEUM OF THE PRADO): Four Portraits of Women of Rank. – Calvary. – The Woman taken in Adultery. – Magdalen Repentant. – Venus and Adonis. – Jesus and the Centurion. – The Infant Jesus, St. Lucia and St. Sebastian. – The Martyrdom of St. Genesius. – Jesus in the Midst of the Doctors. – Cain wandering with his Family. – The Sacrifice of Abraham. – The Adoration of the Magi. – Moses saved from the Waters. – Portrait of a Venetian Woman in Mourning. – Young Man between Vice and Virtue. – Susannah and the two Elders.

GERMANY

DRESDEN (GALLERY): Christ on the Cross. – Moses saved from the Waters. – The Rape of Europa. – The Wedding at Cana (reduced size). – Christ and the two Thieves. – The Good Samaritan. – The Adoration of the Magi. – Portraits of Daniele Barbaro (replica). – The Presentation at the Temple. – Christ cures the Servant of Caharnaum. – Jesus carrying the Cross. – The Resurrection of Christ. – The Adoration of the Virgin.

BERLIN (MUSEUM): Jupiter, Fortune and Germany. – Mars and Minerva. – Apollo and Juno. – Jupiter, Juno, Cybile and Neptune. – Christ and the two Angels. – Four canvases representing Geniuses. – Saturn and Olympe.

MUNICH (PINACOTHEK): Faith and Religion. – The Death of Cleopatra. – Woman taken in Adultery. – Portrait of a Woman. – Justice and Prudence. – The Rest in Egypt. – Love holding chained Dogs. – A Mother and three Children. – Strength and Temperance. – Holy Family. – The Cure of the Servant of Caharnaum.

AUSTRIA

VIENNA (BELVEDERE): The Rape of Dejanire. – Catherine Cornaro. – Christ and the Woman taken in Adultery. – Christ and the Samaritan Woman. – The Adoration of the Magi. – The Marriage of St Catherine. – The Resurrection. – St. Nicholas. – Quintus Curtius throwing himself into the Chasm. – Portrait of Marco Antonio Barbaro. – Young Man caressing a Dog. – Annunciation to the Virgin. – Adam and Eve and their First-born. – Venus and Adonis. – St. Sebastian. – The Death of Lucrece. – St John the Baptist – Judith. – Christ entering the House of Zaira. – St. Catherine and St. Barbara present two Nuns to the Virgin and the Infant Jesus.

SWEDEN

STOCKHOLM (NATIONAL MUSEUM): The Circumcision. – Magdalen. – A Holy Family. – A Madonna.

RUSSIA

ST. PETERSBURG (HERMITAGE): The Flight into Egypt. – The Adoration of the Magi. – Holy Family. – Diana and Minerva. – Mars and Venus. – Portrait of a Man. – Lazarus and the Rich Man. – Christ in the midst of the Doctors. – The Dead Christ upheld by the Virgin and an Angel. – The Marriage of St. Catherine. – Various Sketches.

LEUCHTEMBERG GALLERY: The Adoration of the Magi. – The Widow of the Spanish Ambassador at Venice presenting her Son to Philip II.

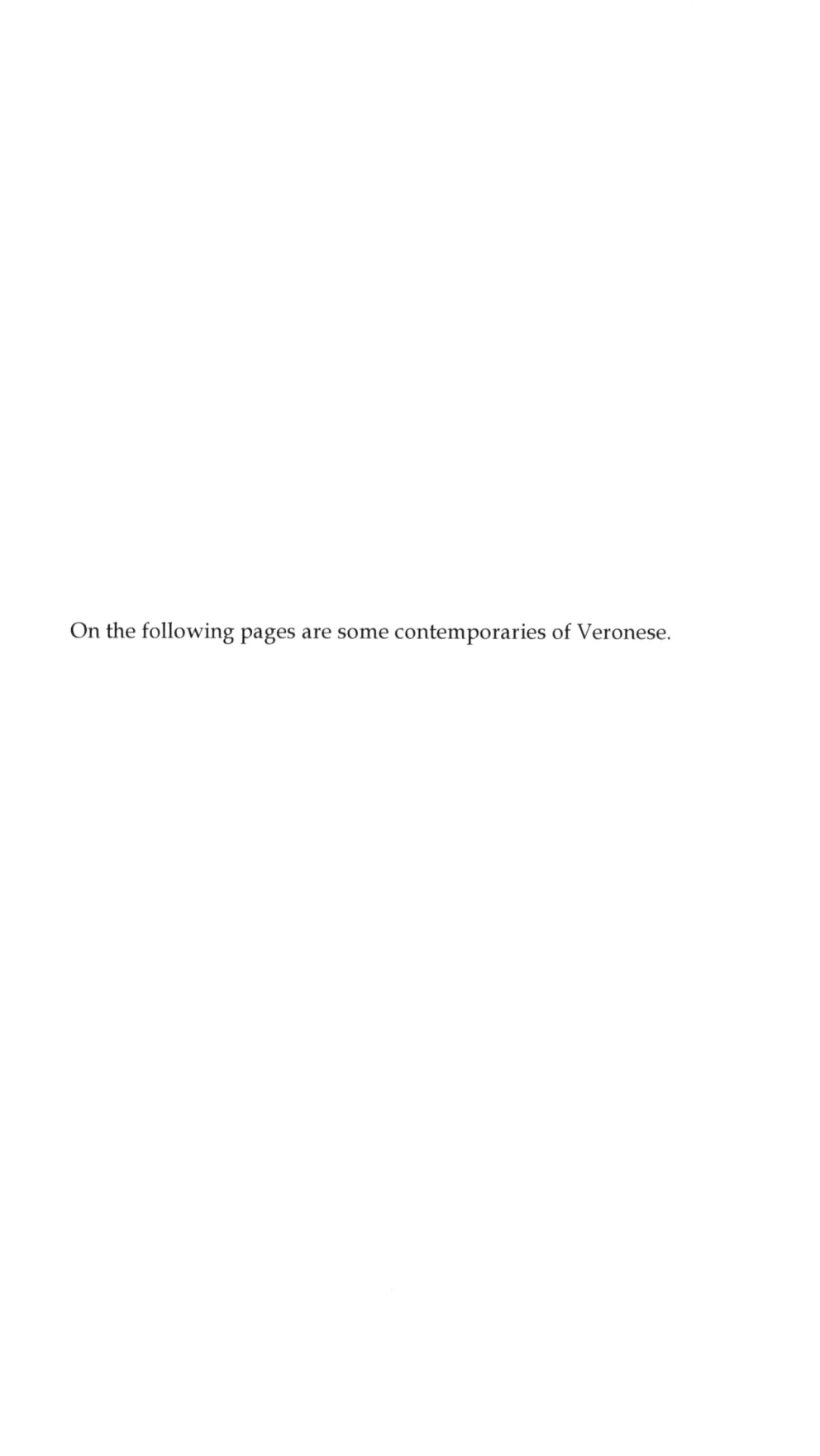

On the following pages are some contemporaries of Veronese.

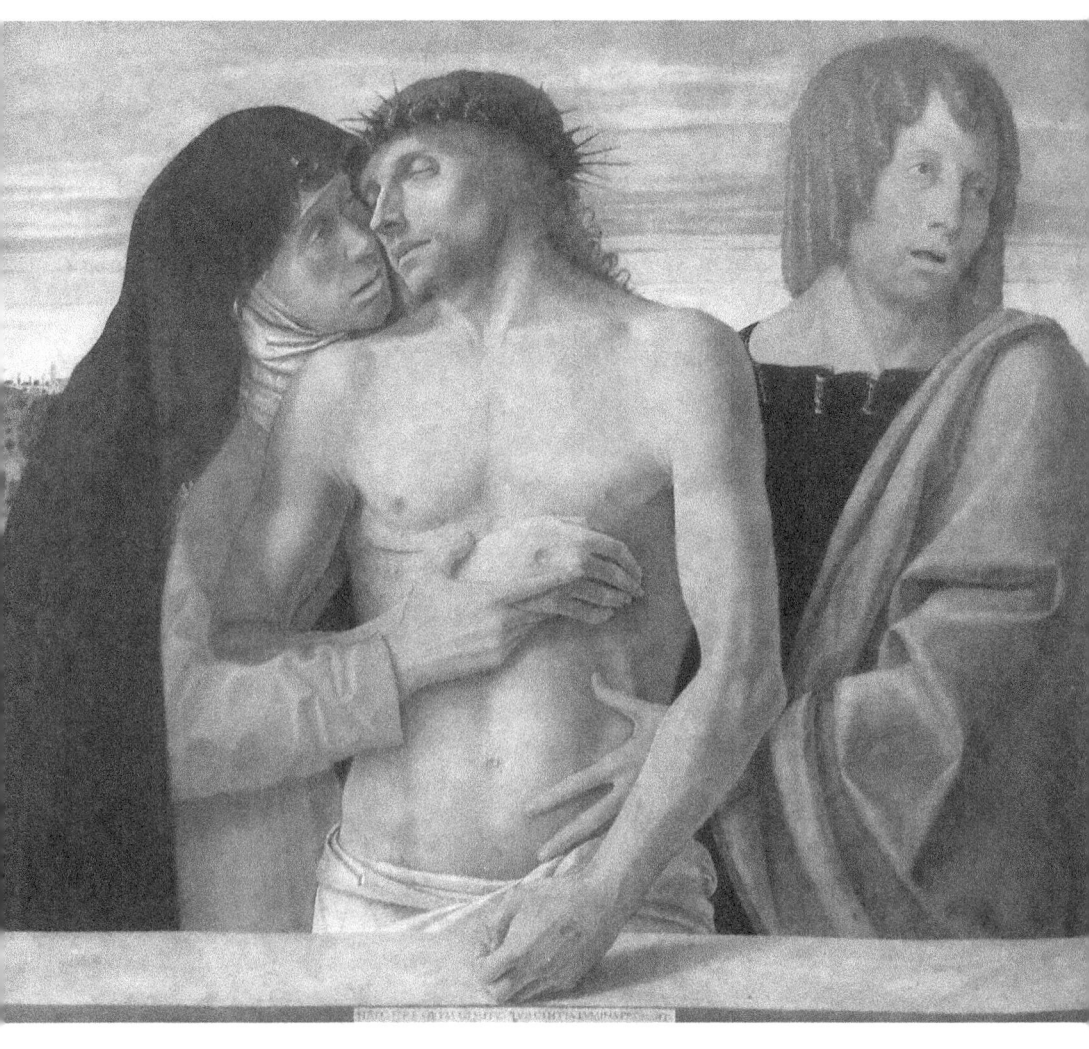

Giovanni Bellini, Pietà, Milan

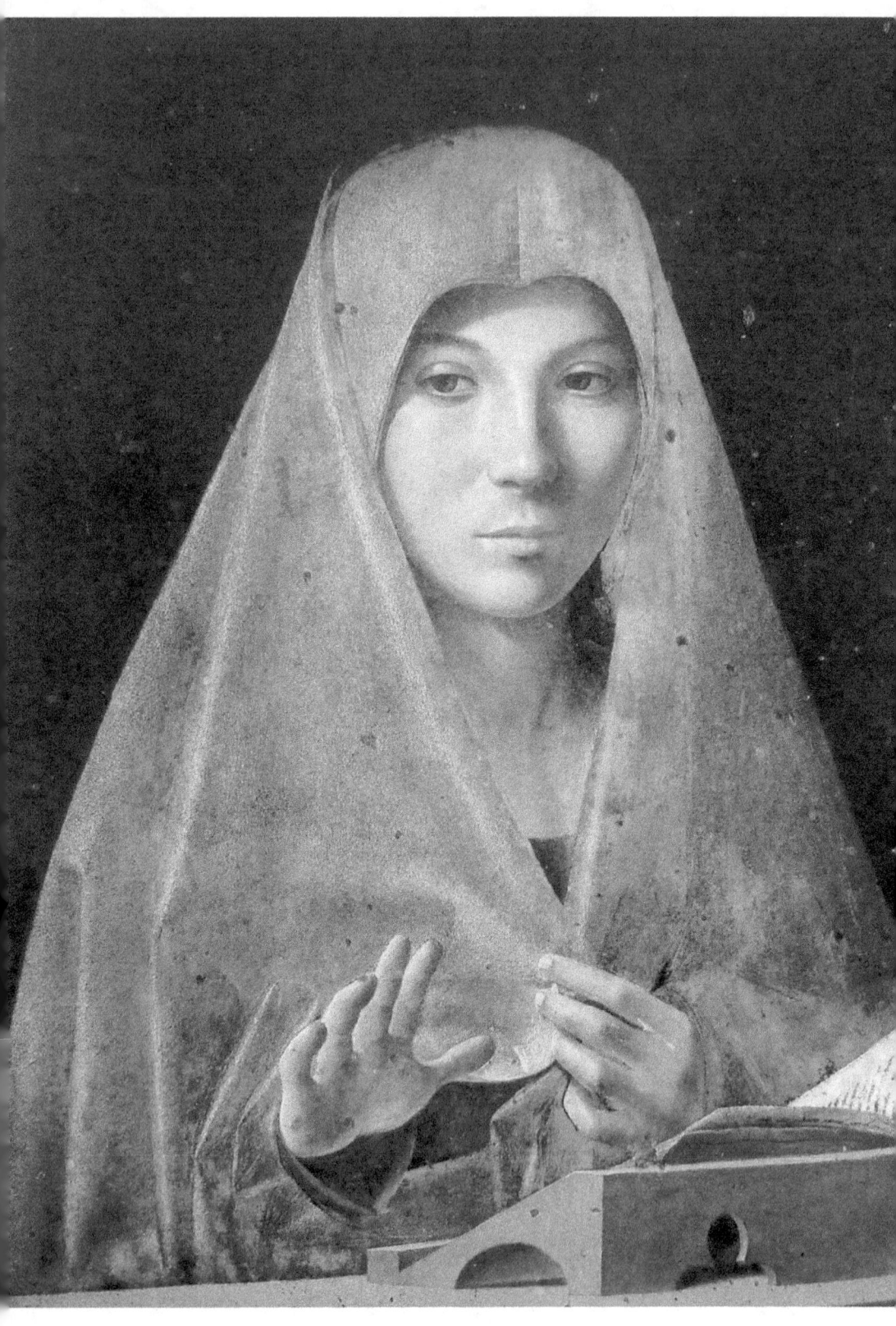

Antonello da Messina, The Virgin of the Annunciation, 1475, Palermo

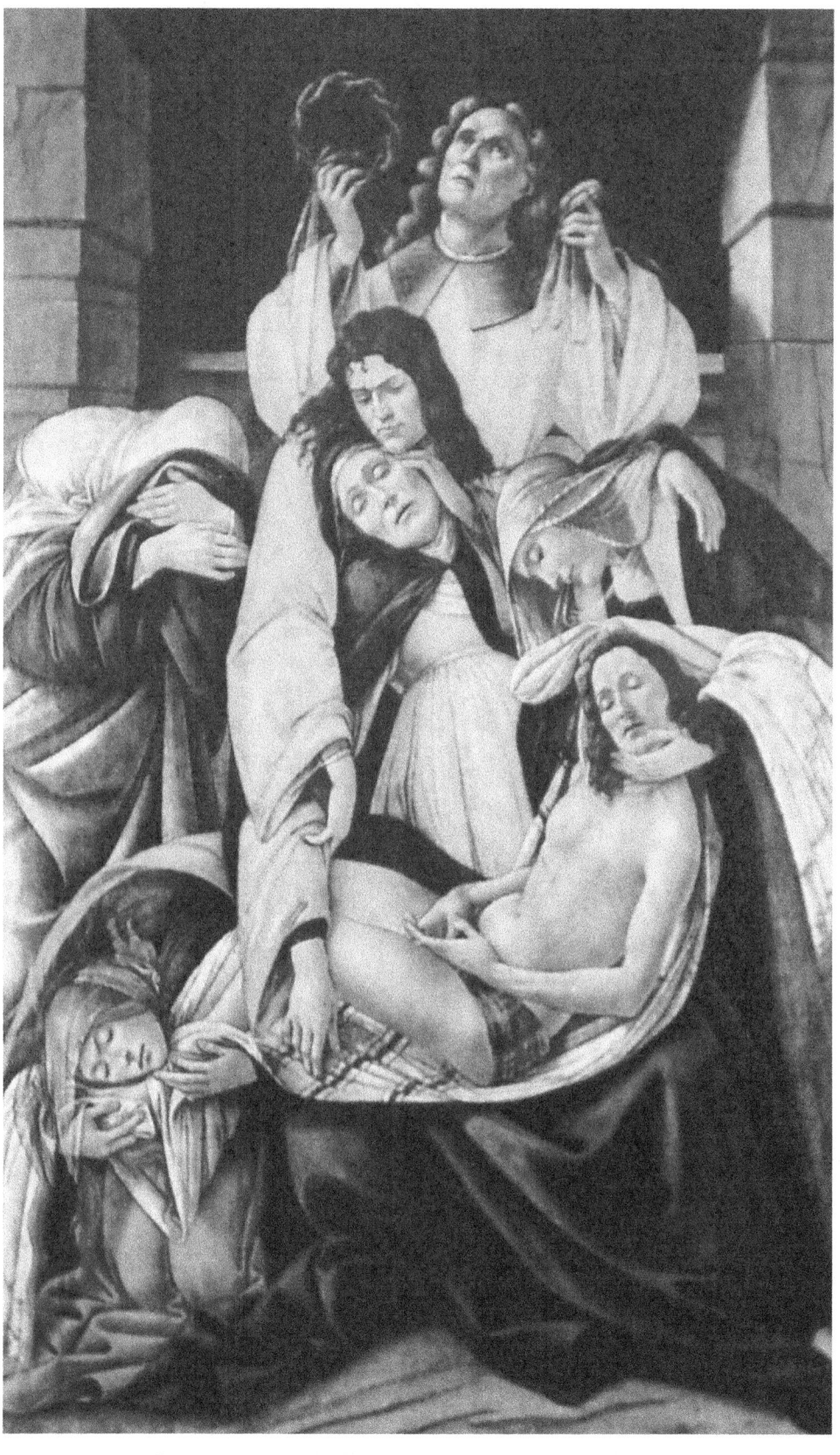

Sandro Botticelli, *Pietà*, Museo Poldi Pezzoli, Milan

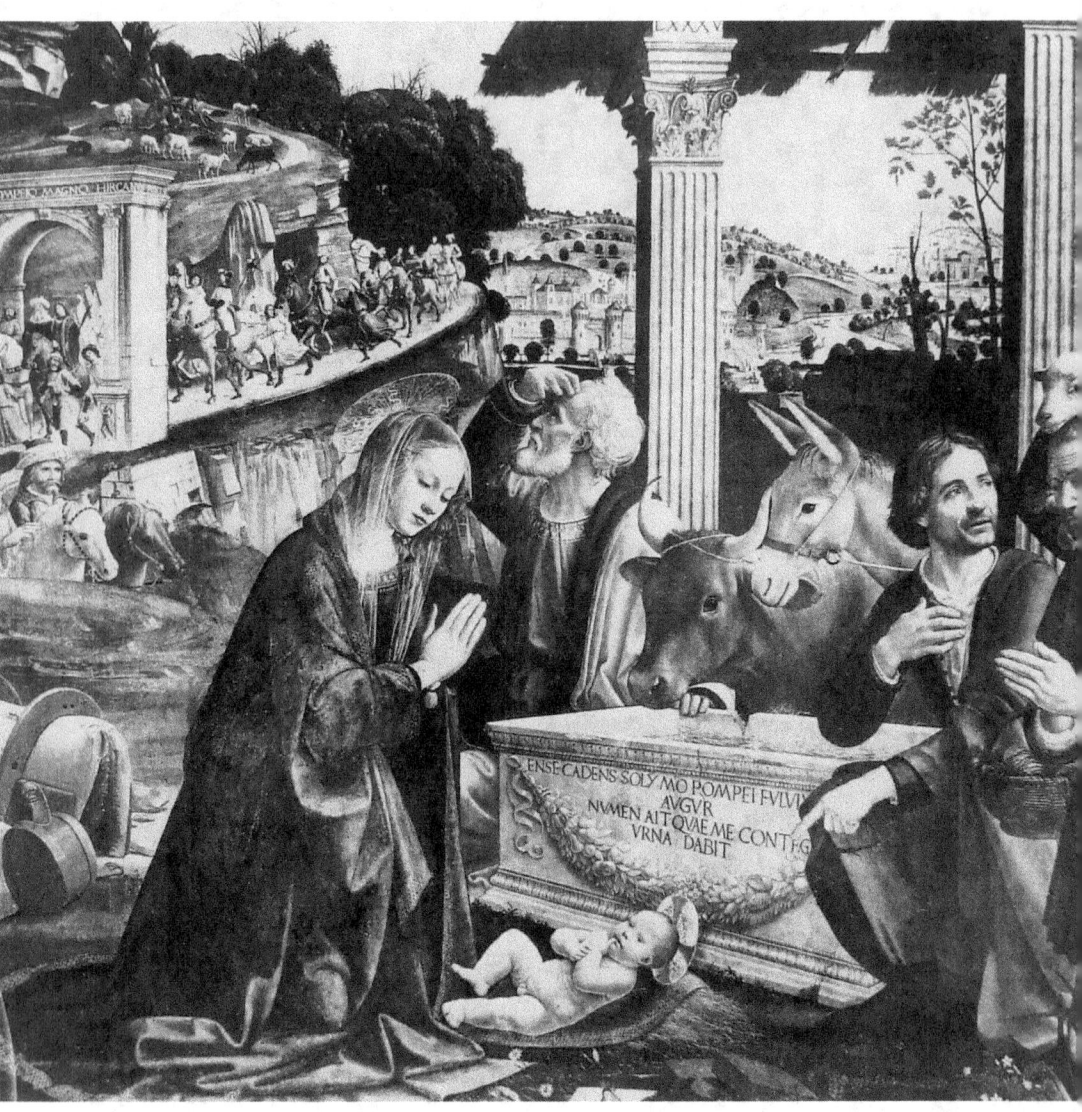

Domenico Ghirlandaio, Adoration of the Shepherds, 1485

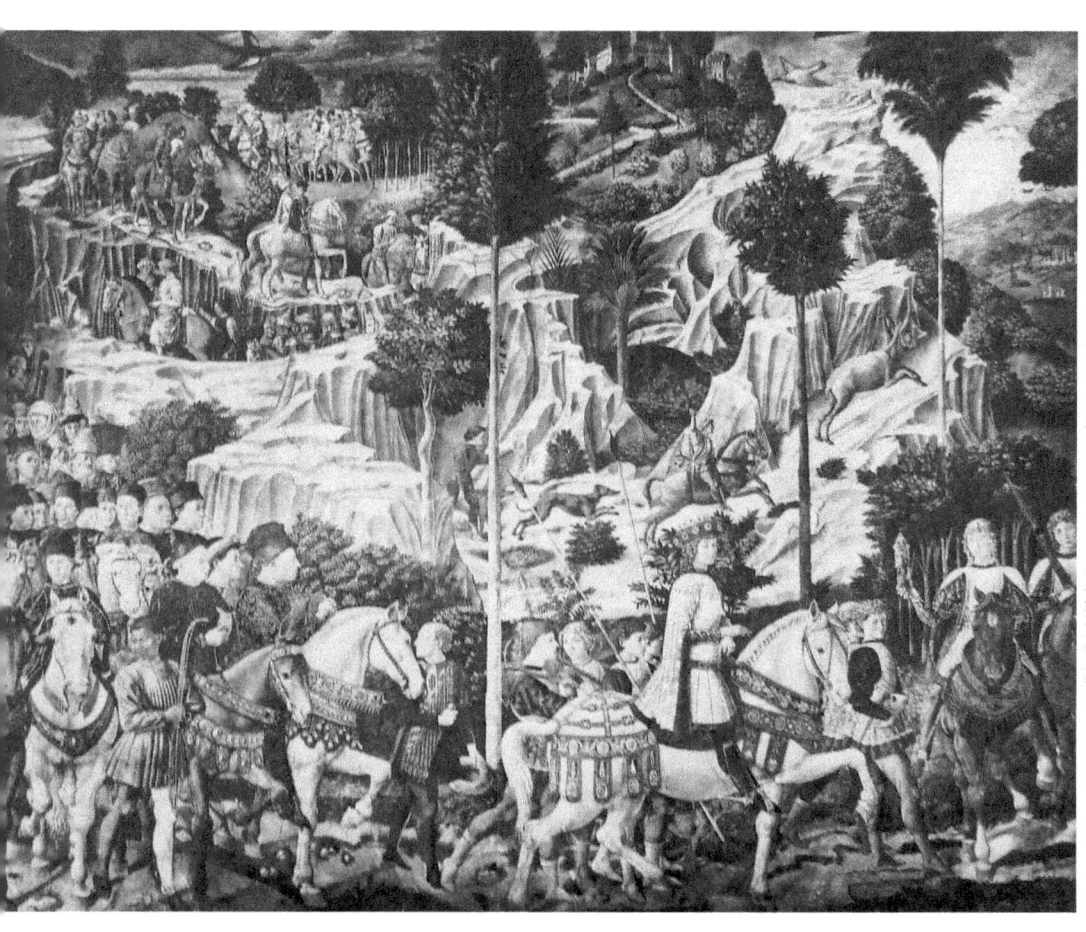

Benozzo Gozzoli, Journey of the Magi

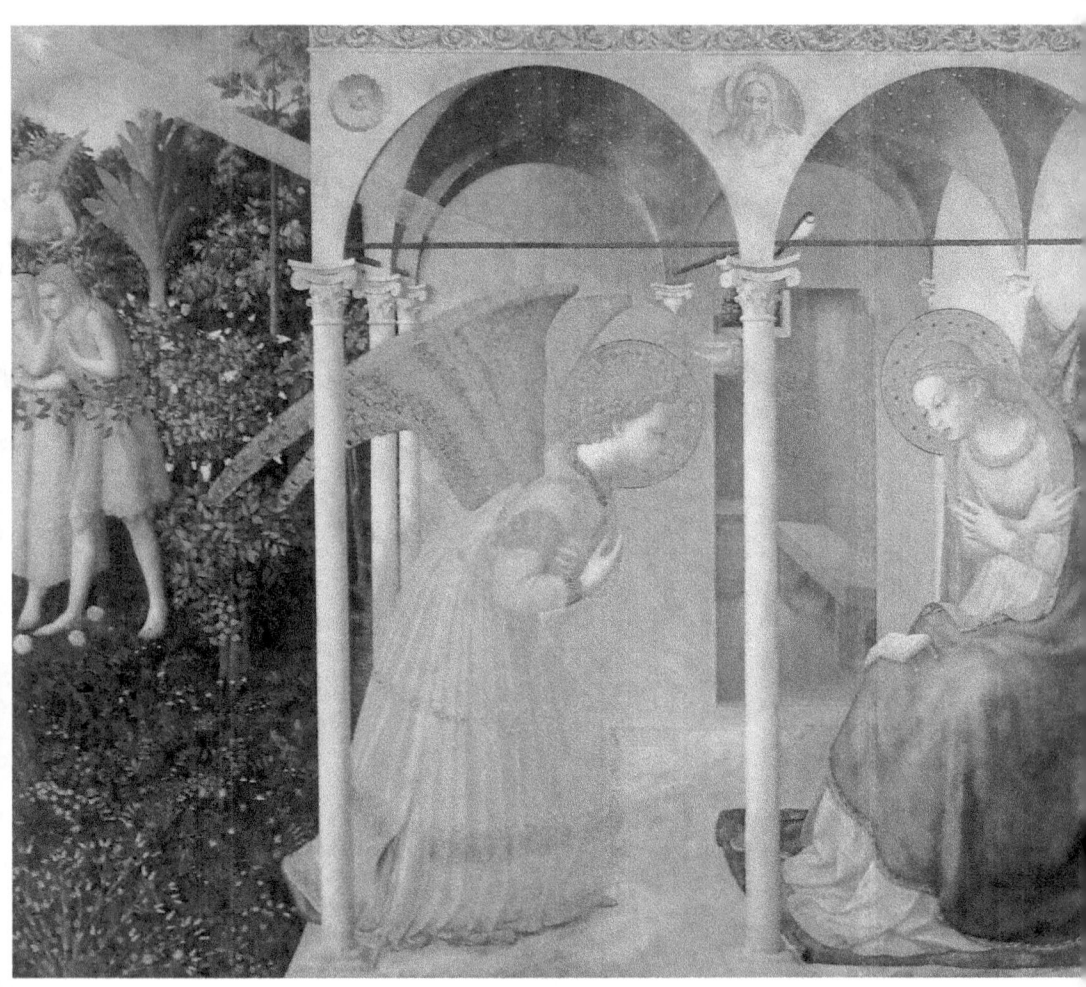

Fra Angelico, Annunciation, Prado, Madrid

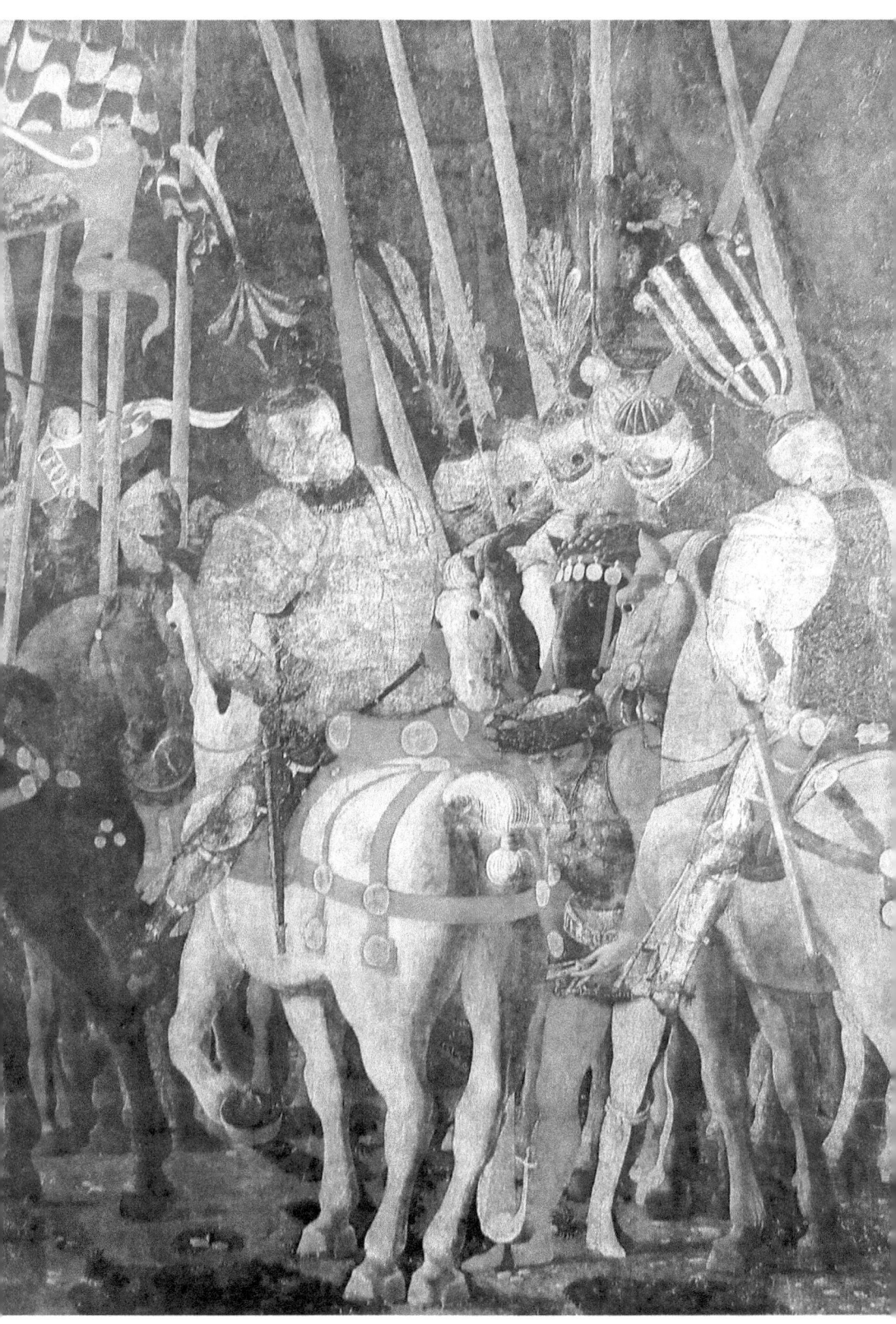

Paolo Uccello, The Battle of San Romano, Paris

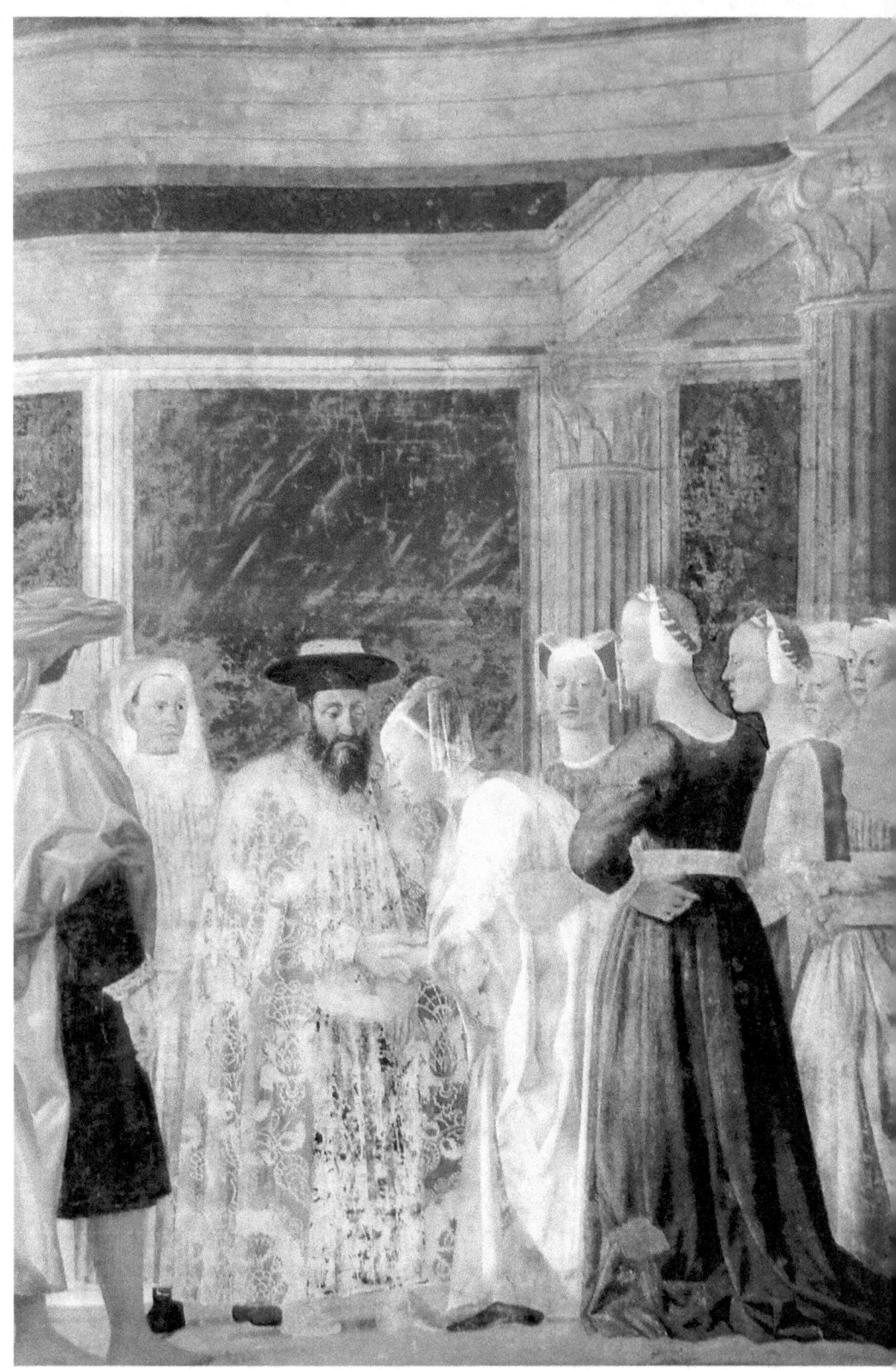

Piero della Francesca, frescoes, Arezzo

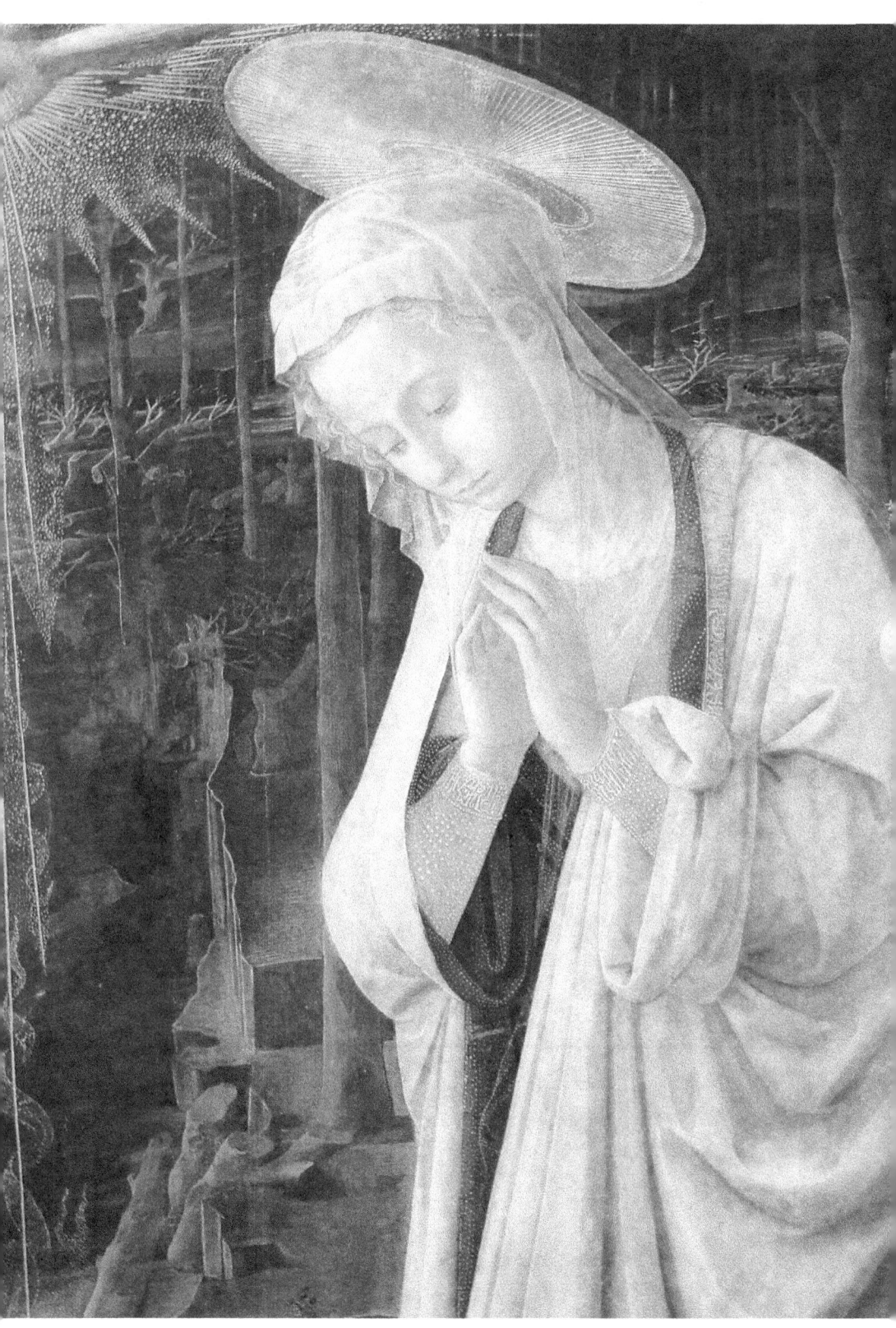

Fra Filippo Lippi, The Adoration of the Virgin, Berlin, detail

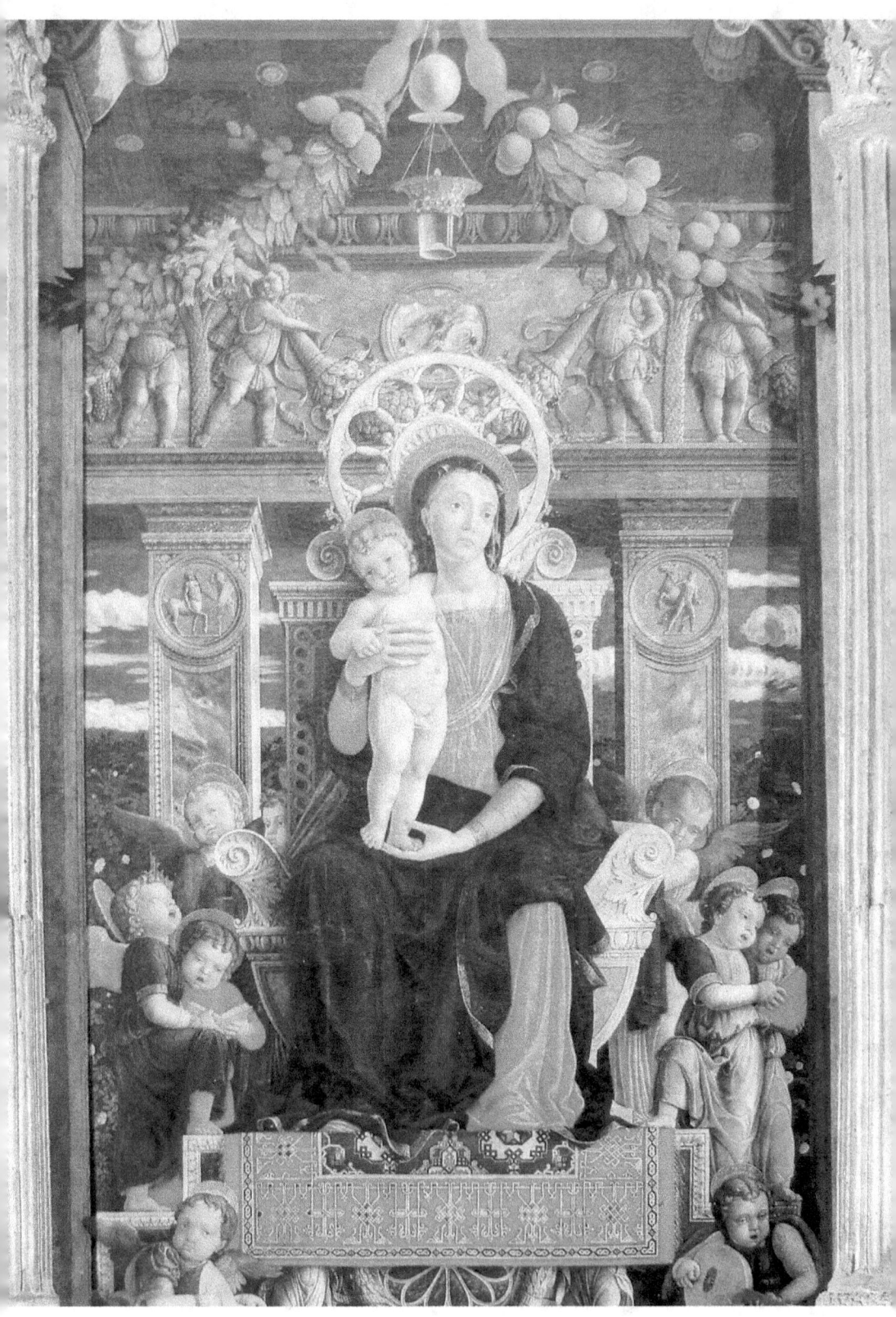

Andreas Mantegna, Madonna and Child Enthroned, 1457-60, Verona

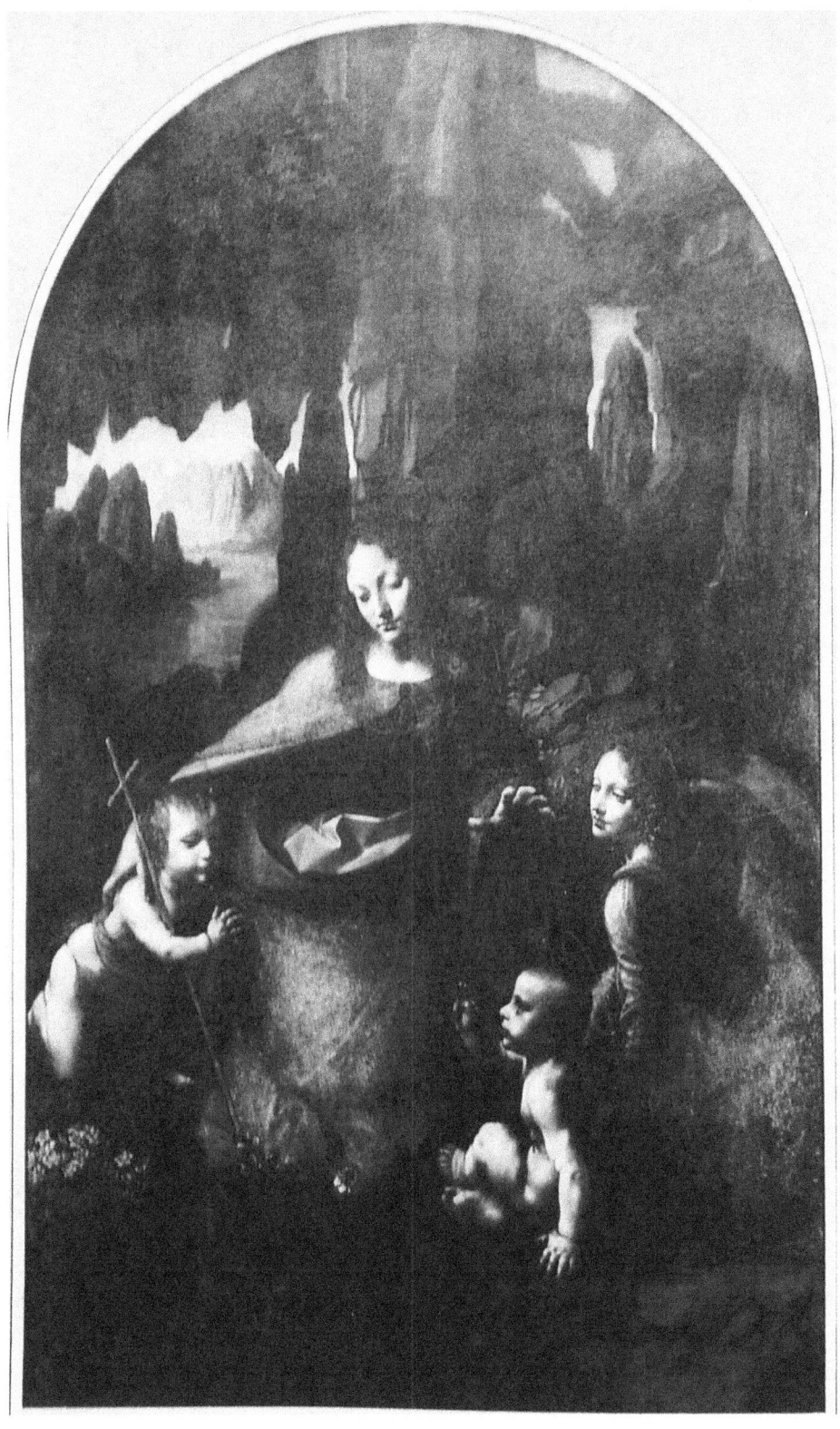

Leonardo da Vinci, The Madonna of the Rocks, London

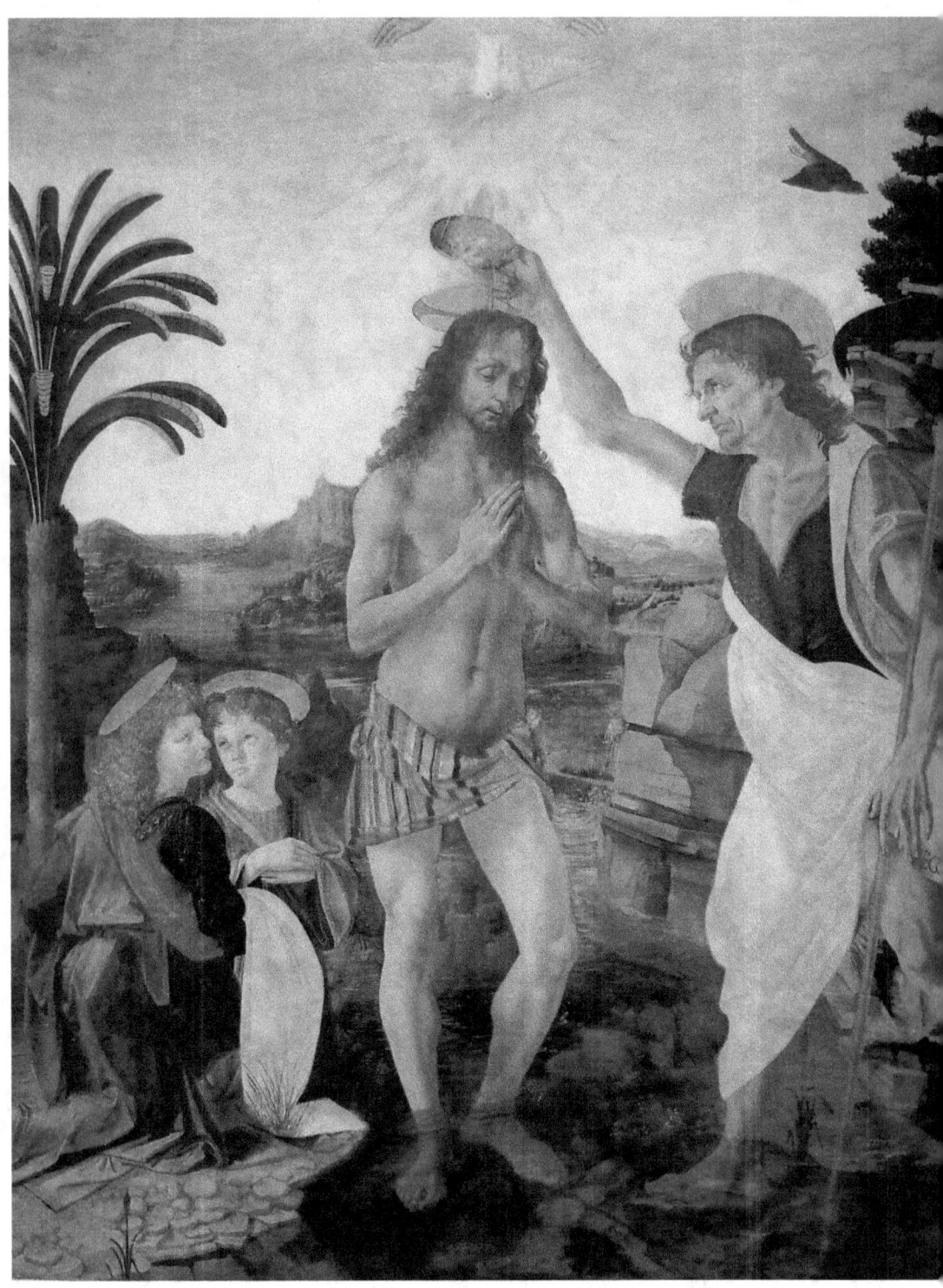

Andrea del Verrocchio, The Baptism of Christ

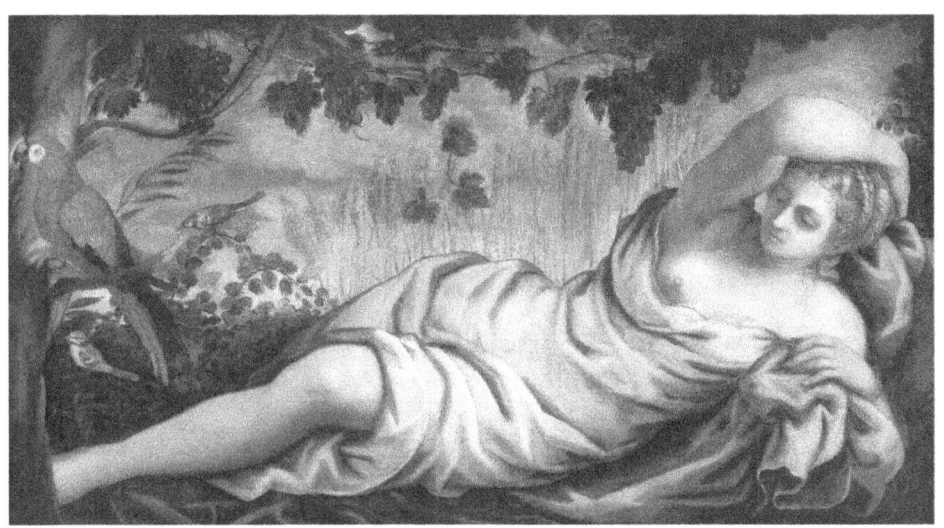

Tintoretto, Summer, 1555, Washington, DC

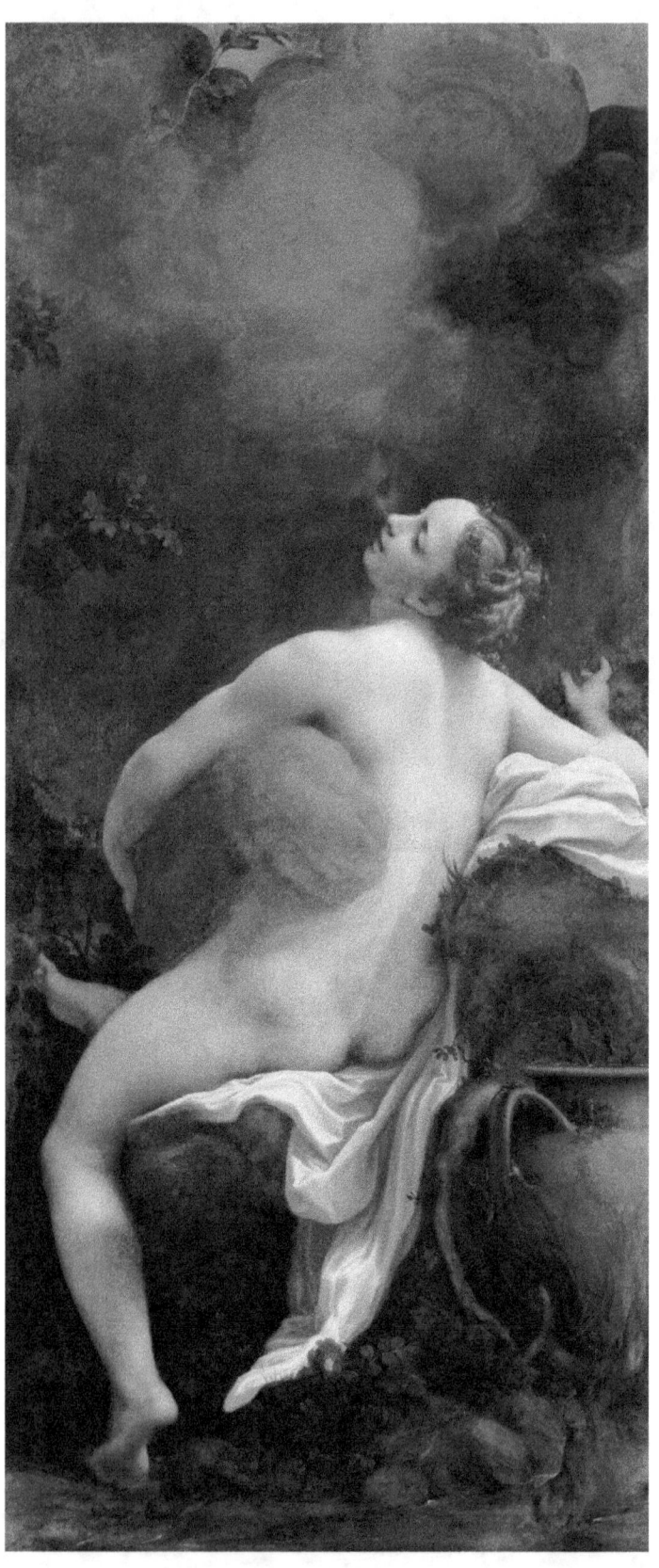

Correggio,
Jupiter and Antiope

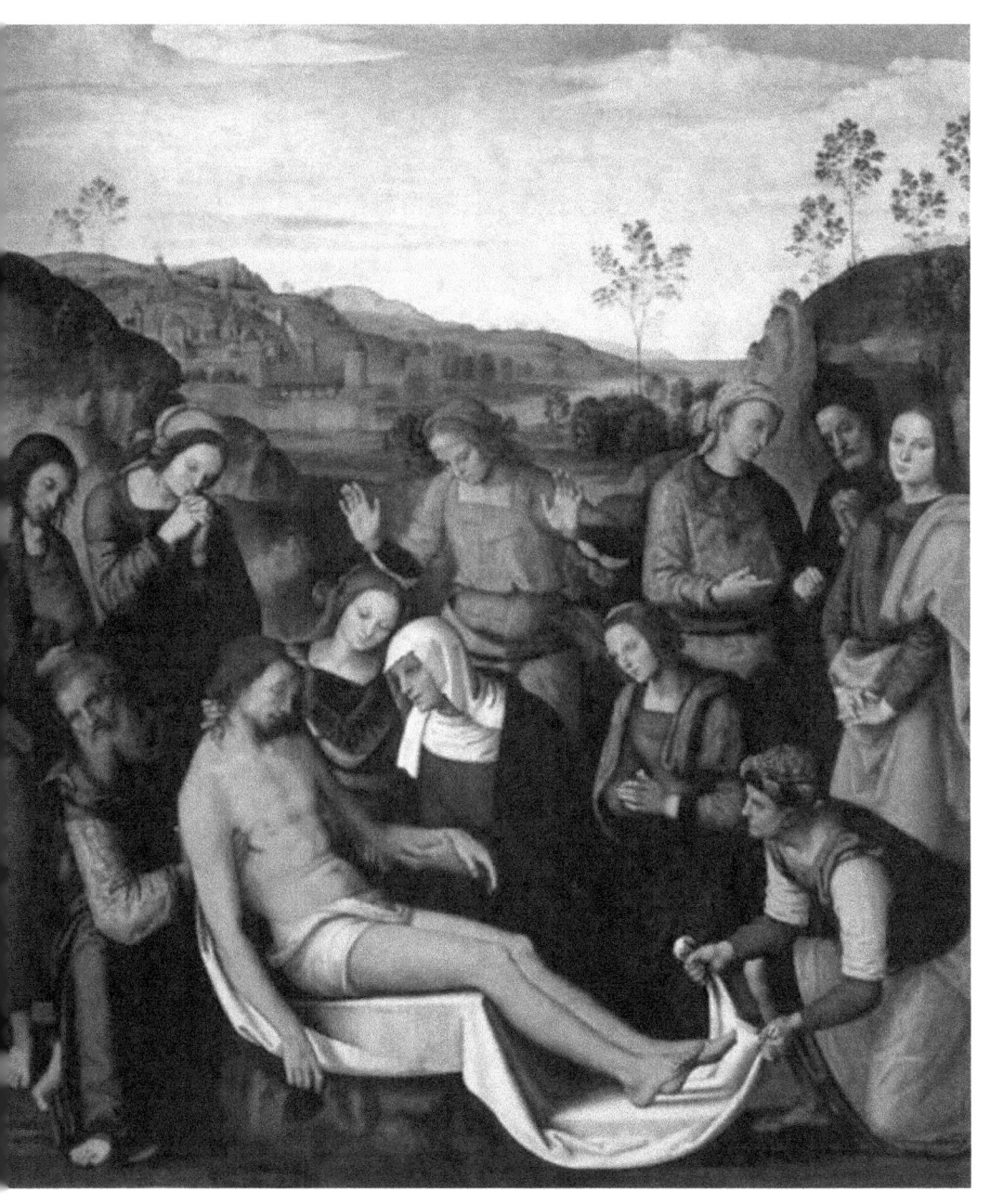

Perugino, The Mourning of the Dead Christ, 1495

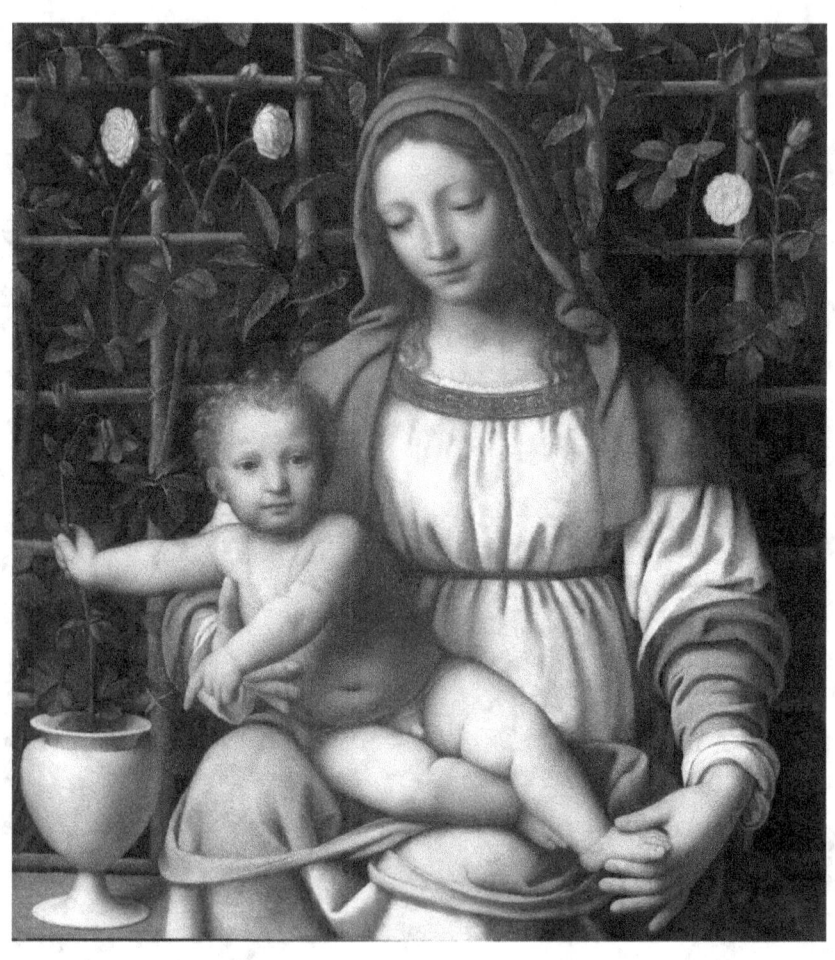

Bernardino Luini, Madonna and Child, Milan

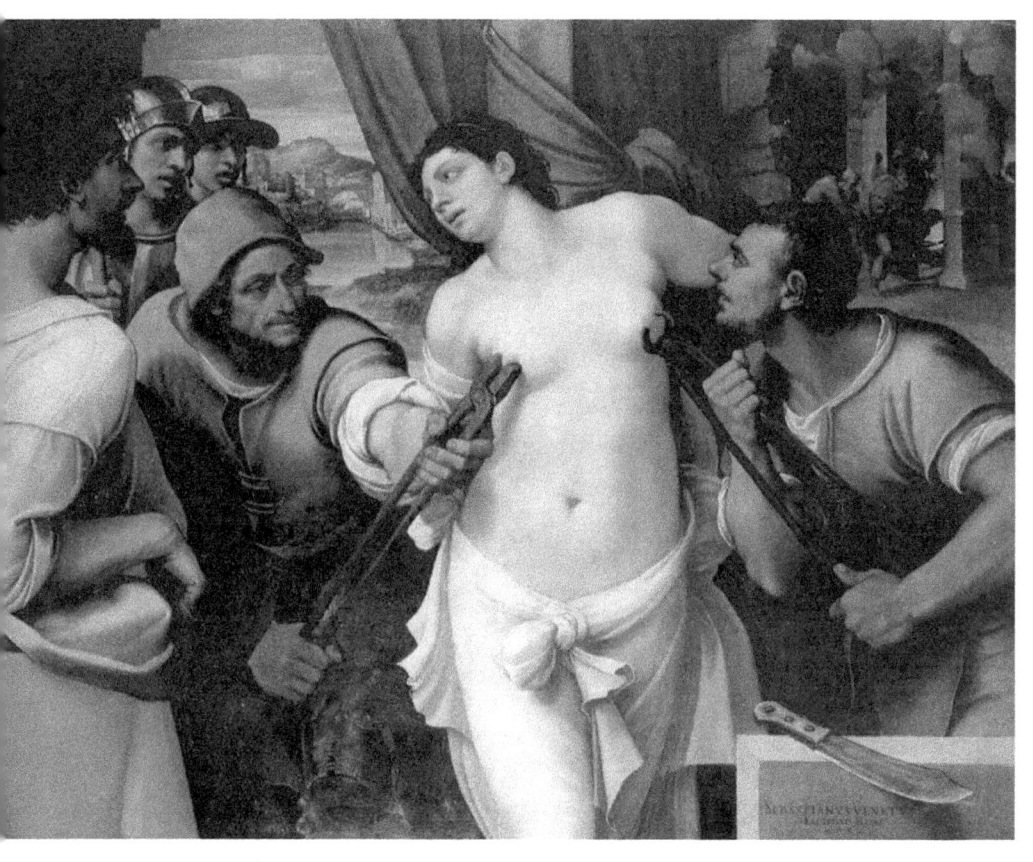

Sebastiano del Piombo, The Martyrdom of St Agatha, 1520,
Pitti Palace, Florence

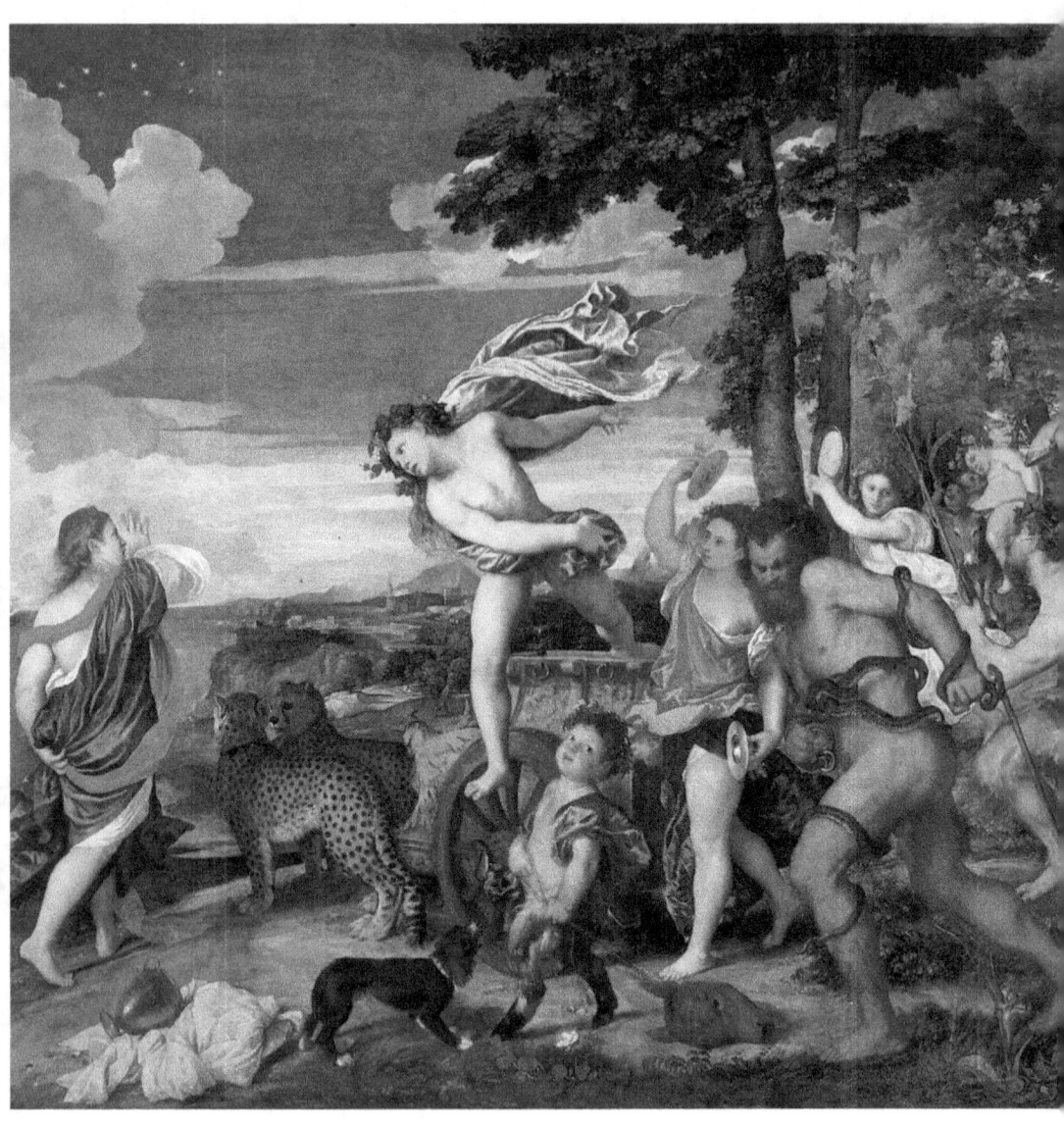

Titian, Bacchus and Ariadne, 1520-23, London

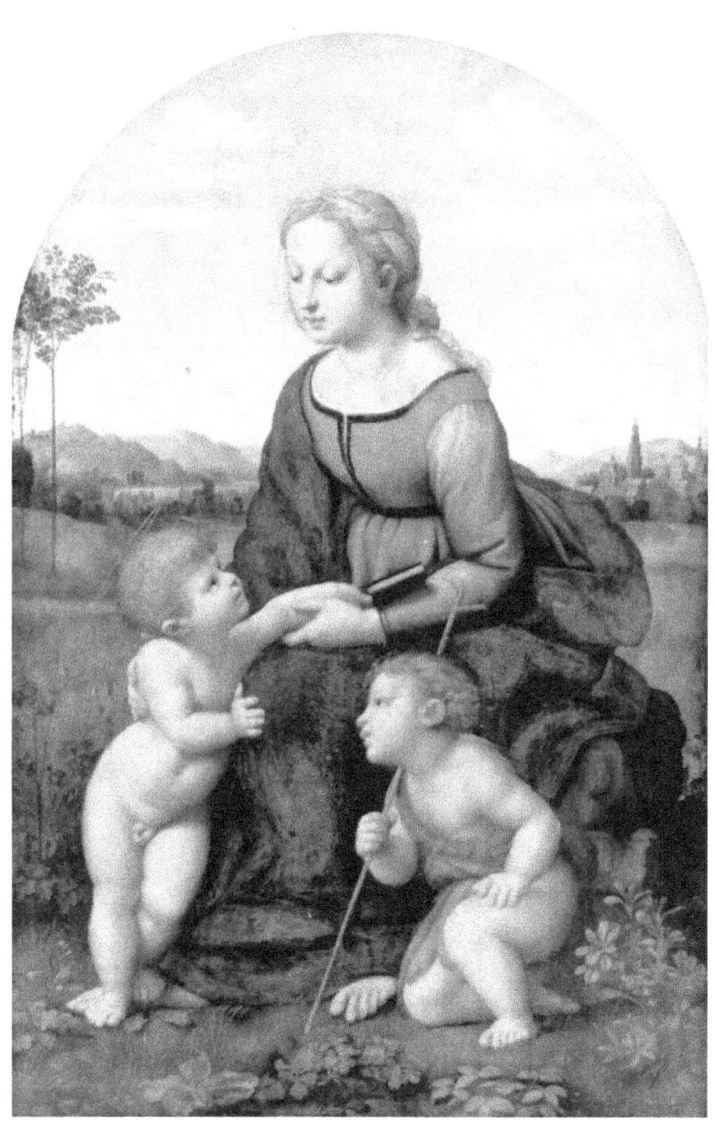

Raphael, La Belle Jardiniere, 1507, Louvre

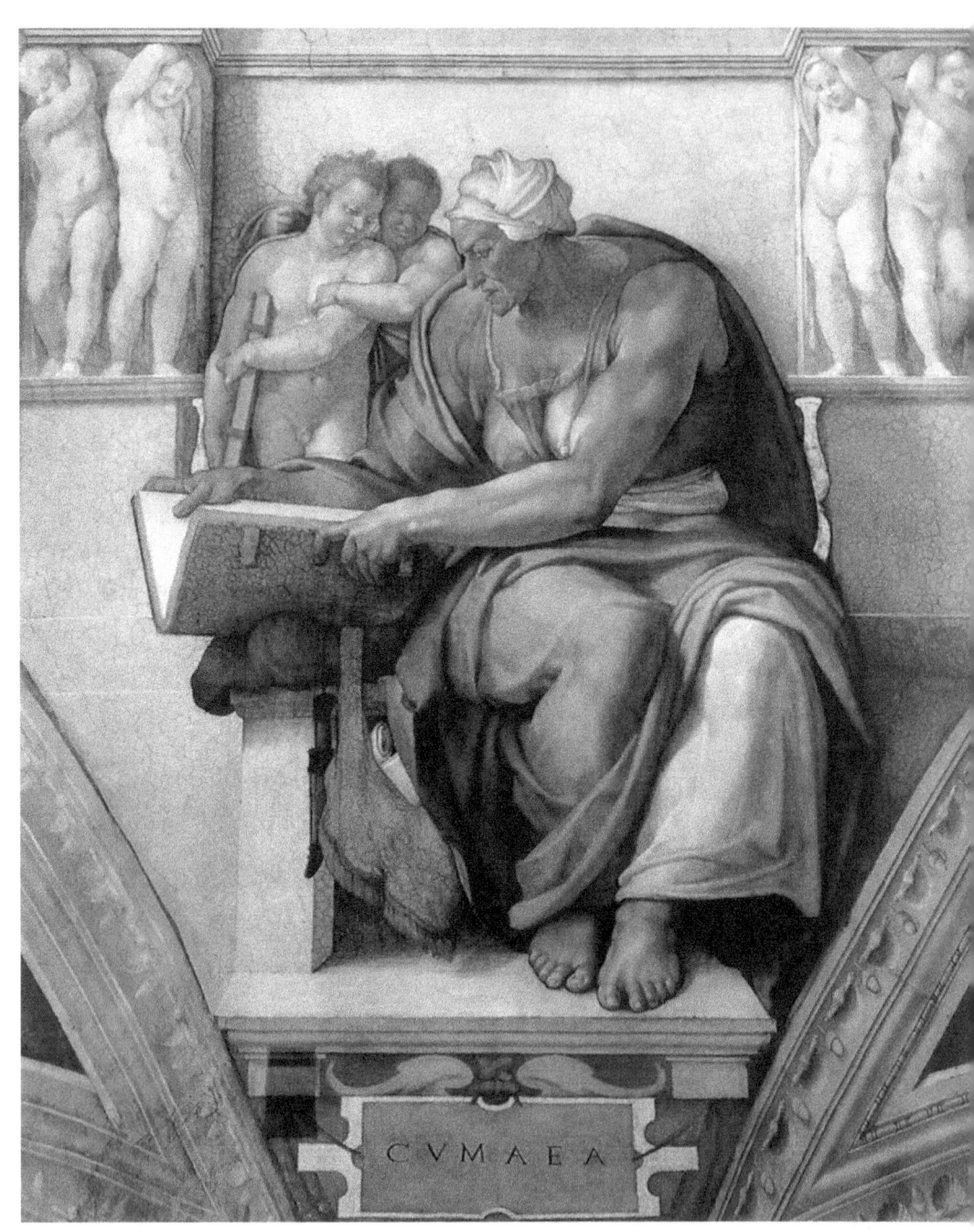

Michelangelo, Cumaean Sibyle, Sistine Chapel.

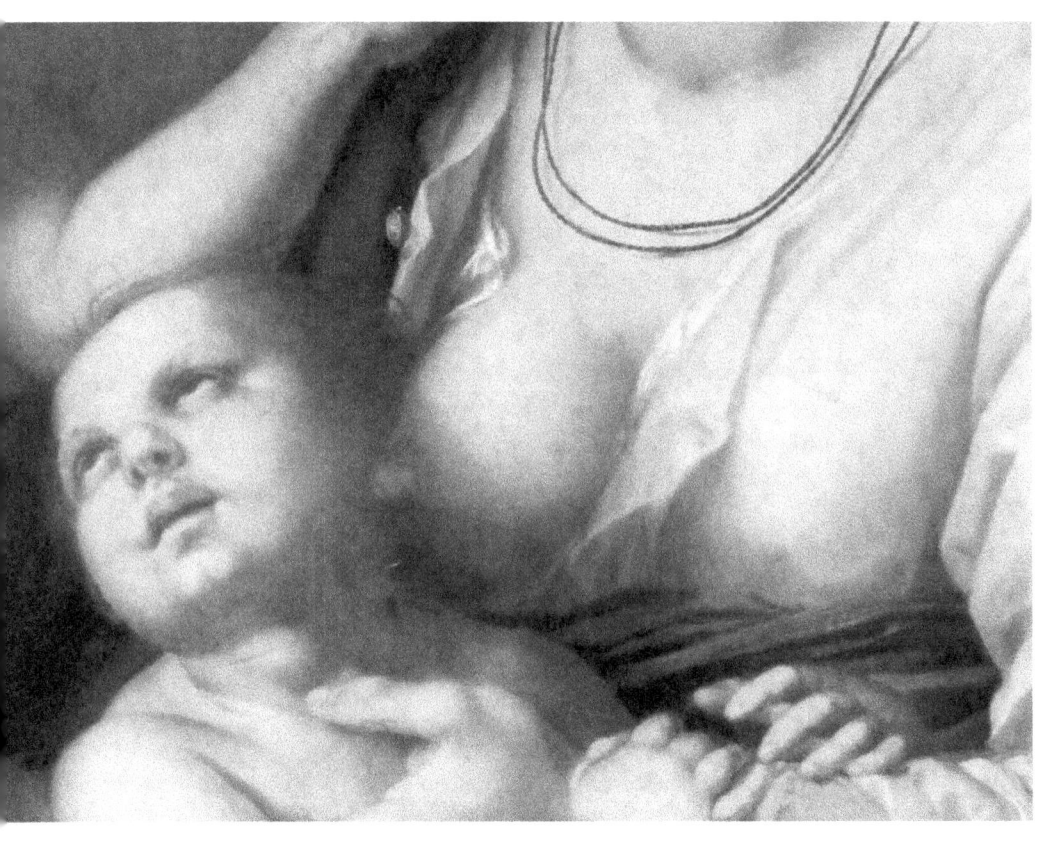

Andrea del Sarto, Madonna and Child, detail

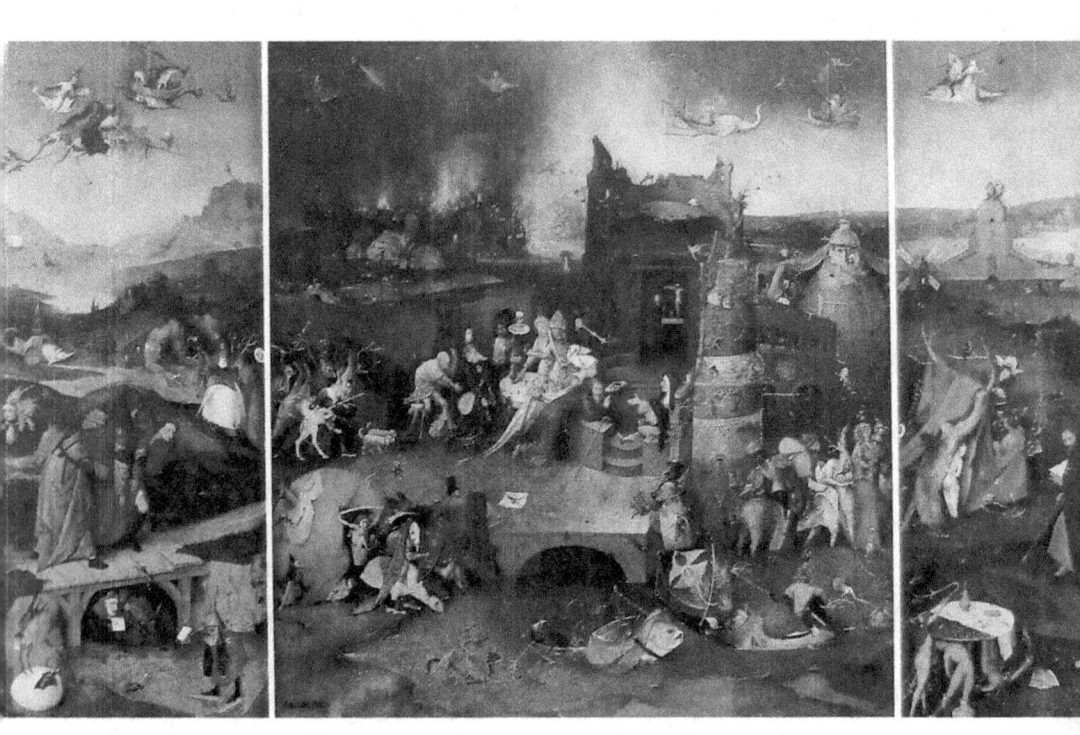

Hieronymous Bosch, The Temptations of St Anthony

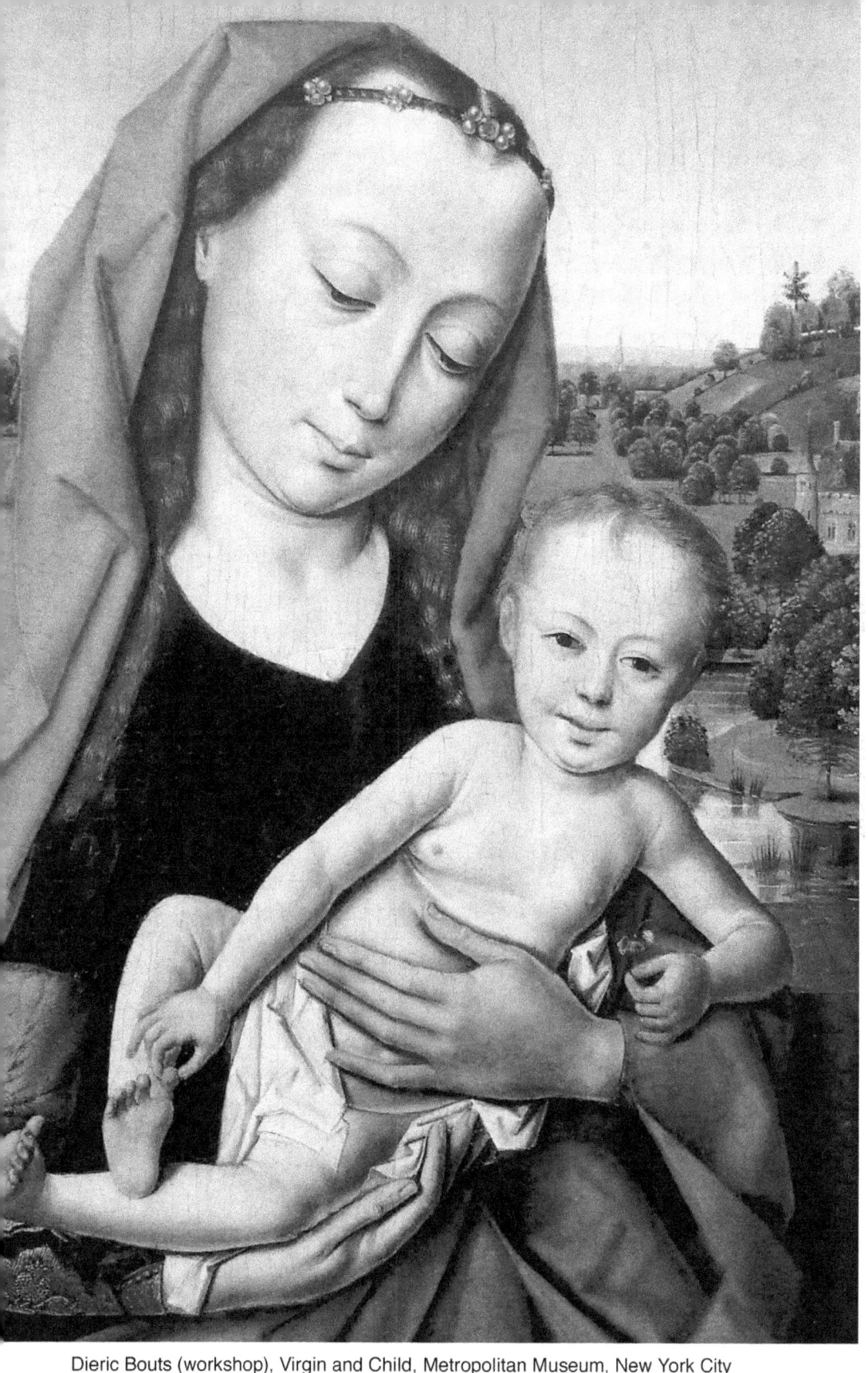

Dieric Bouts (workshop), Virgin and Child, Metropolitan Museum, New York City

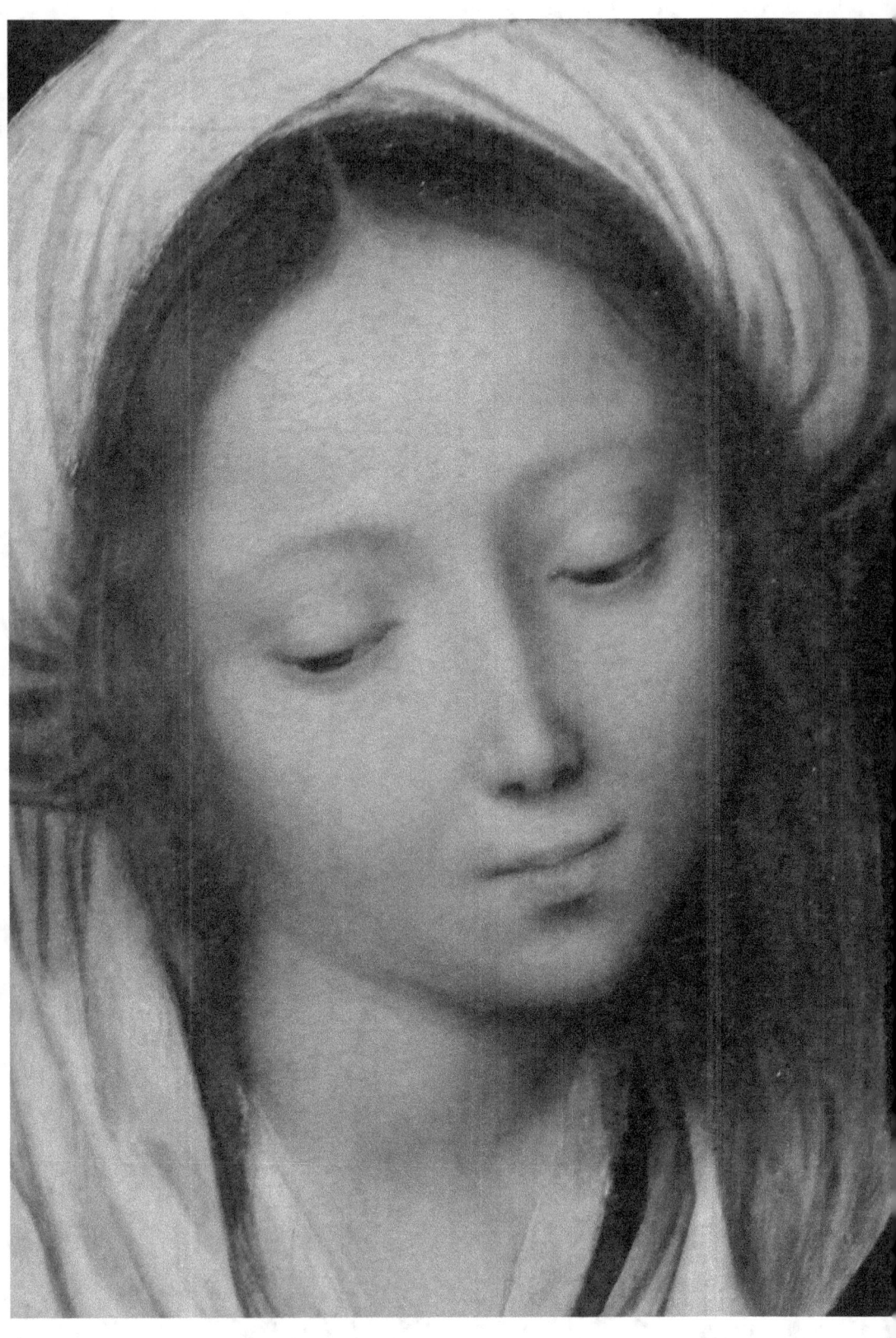

Gerard David, detail of the Adoration, Metropolitan Museum of Art

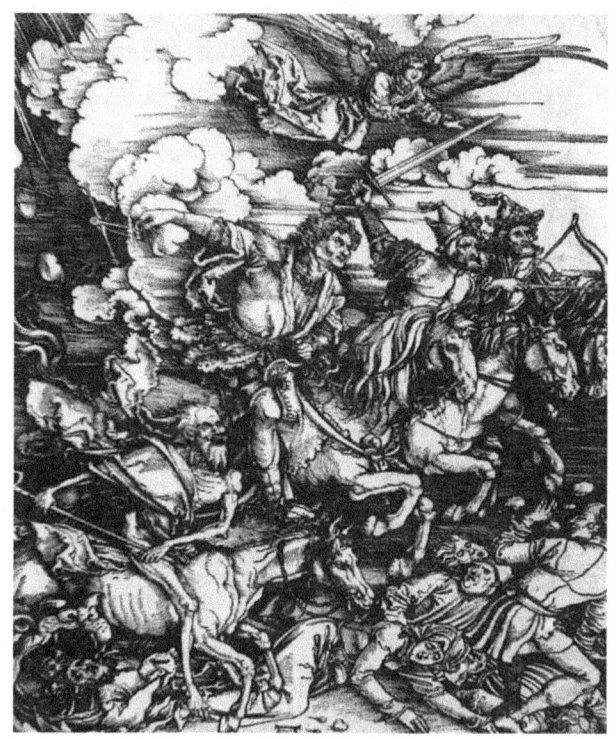

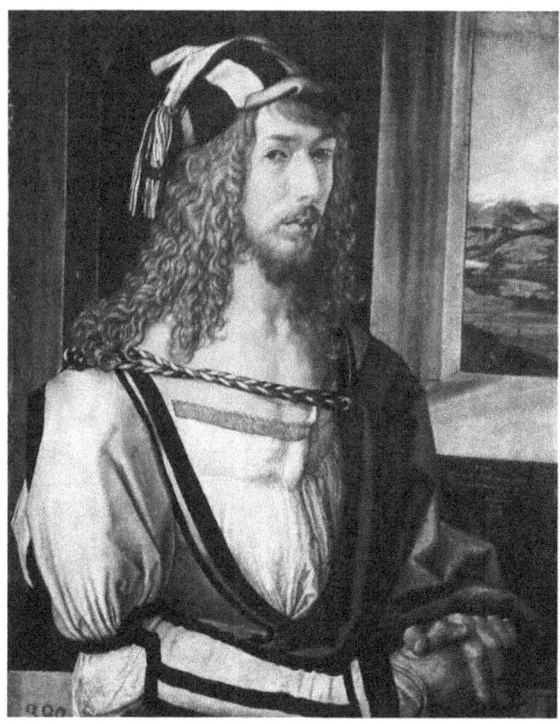

Albrecht Dürer

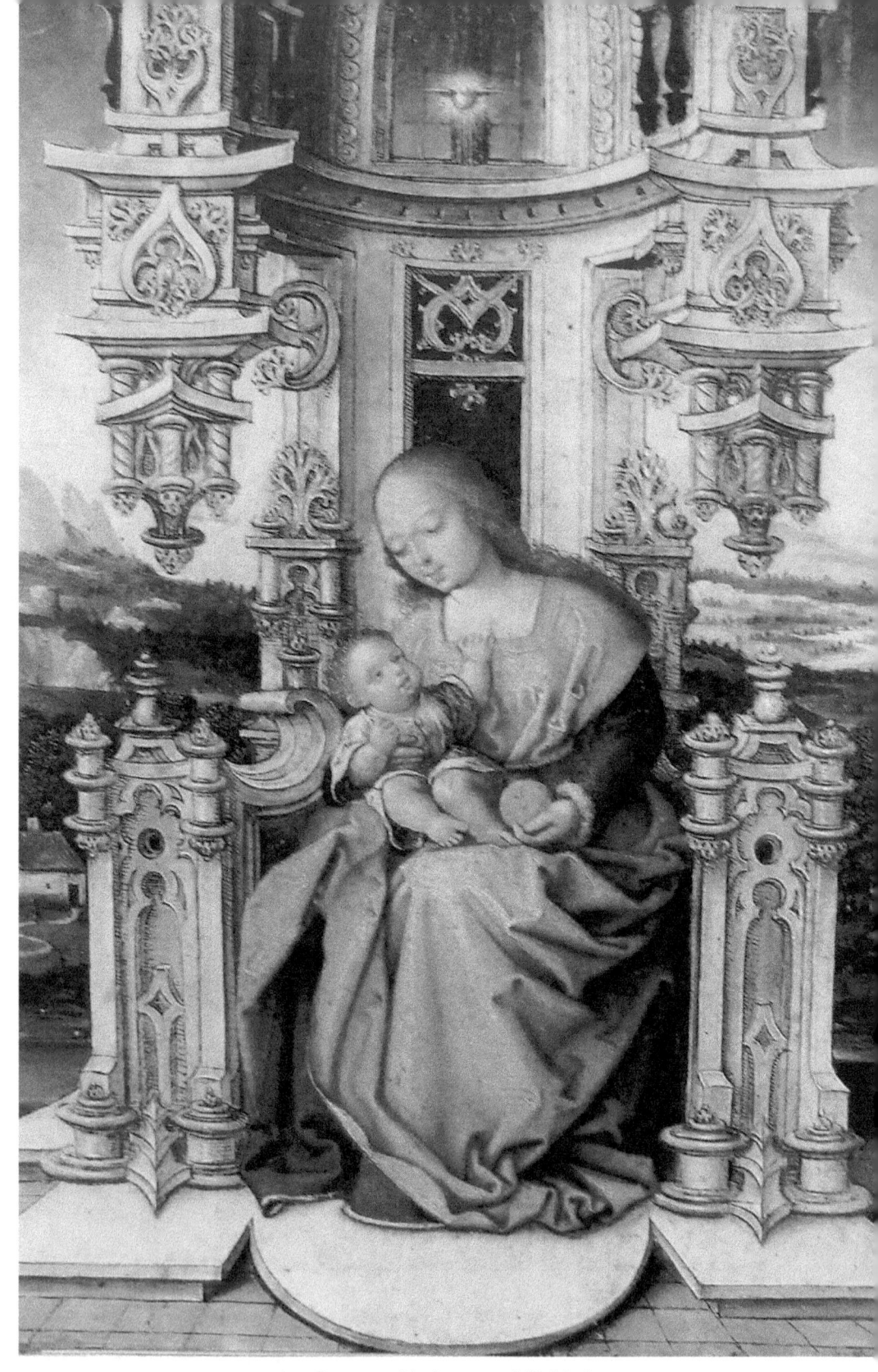

Jan Gossaert, Madonna and Child, Antwerp

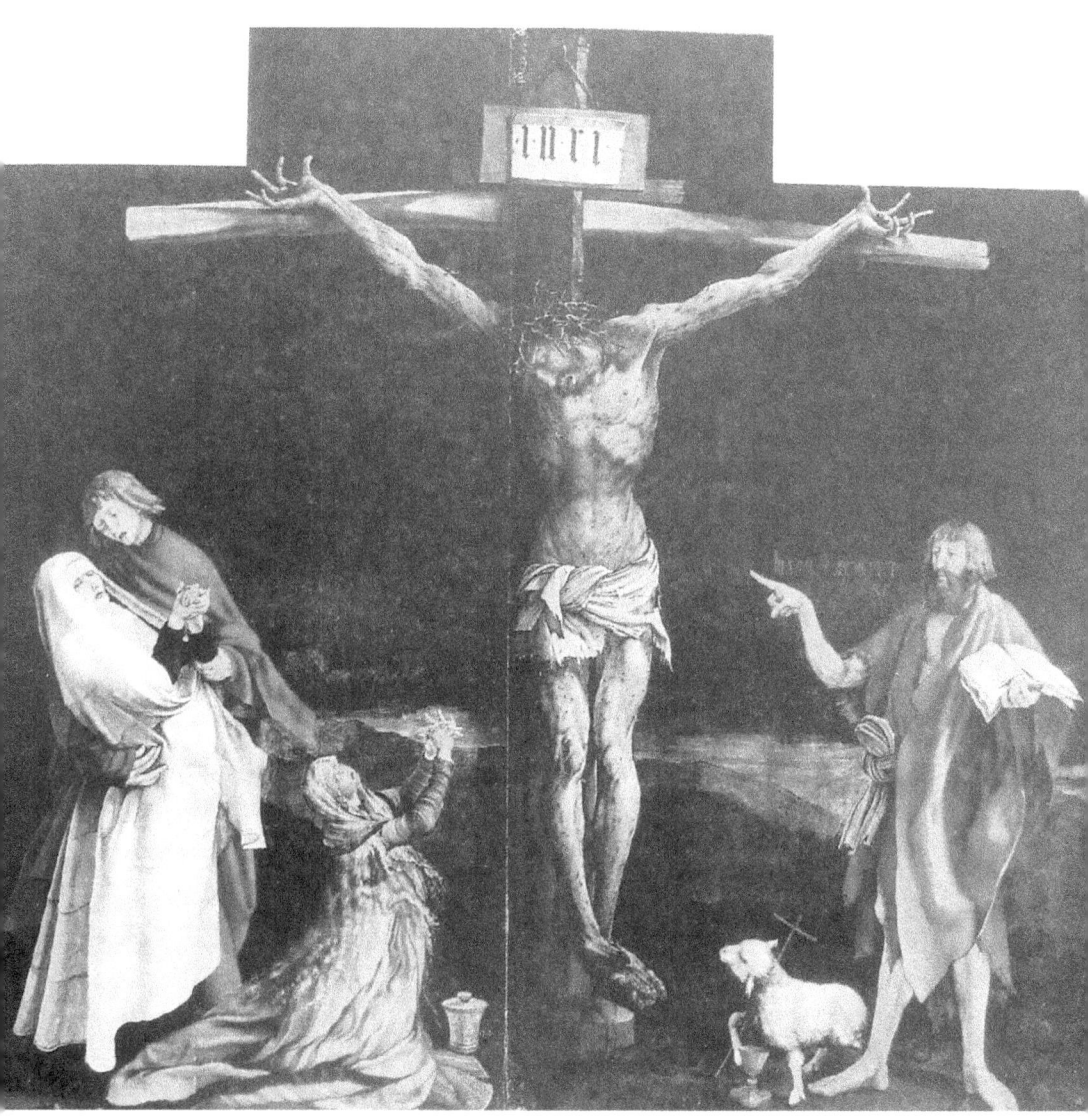

Matthias Grünewald, Crucifixion, Isenheim Altarpiece

NOTES ON WORKS

JUPITER DESTROYING THE VICES
(In the Musée du Louvre)

This large composition shows a method rarely employed by Veronese. The great imaginative artist here tried his hand at the more vigorous school of painting, and with complete success. It is especially admired for certain remarkable effects of foreshortening. This picture, painted for the Ducal Palace, served as a ceiling decoration in Louis XIVth's chamber at Versailles, until it was finally transferred to the Louvre.

THE DISCIPLES AT EMMAUS
(In the Musée du Louvre)

This biblical scene, as treated by Veronese, in no wise resembles the same subject as treated by the Primitives or by Rembrandt. The Venetian Master does not trouble himself about tradition; for him, this Feast is simply an opportunity for a beautiful picture, brilliant in colour, and embellished with rich accessories and architectural drawing.

THE HOLY FAMILY
(In the Musée du Louvre)

In this work, one of the most beautiful in the Salon Carré, Veronese has grouped his figures in a charming manner. Following his customary formula, he has clothed them in the Venetian style, but the faces of the Virgin and the Child are remarkable for their tenderness. It is a matter of regret that time has faded the colours of this magnificent painting.

THE WEDDING AT CANA
(In the Musée du Louvre)

This immense composition is the most celebrated work by Veronese. It is considered as one of the masterpieces of all painting. The greater number of the guests at this feast are portraits of illustrious characters of the sixteenth century, and the artist has included himself, along with Tintoretto and Titian, in the group of musicians in the foreground.

THE FAMILY OF DARIUS
(In the National Gallery, London)

This picturesque painting is one of the most curious of all Veronese's works. It was painted in return for the hospitality which he received from the Pisani family, and all the figures in it are portraits of members of the household. Another point worthy of note is the anachronism of the warriors clad in Roman armour standing before the kneeling women, who are dressed in the manner of the sixteenth century.

CALVARY
(In the Musée du Louvre)

In painting this subject, which so many artists have treated in a lugubrious tone, Veronese, while preserving the intense sadness of the scene on Calvary, has none the less succeeded in lavishing upon it his habitual qualities as a colourist. All the actors in the divine drama wear gloomy countenances and resplendent robes.

THE MARRIAGE OF ST. CATHERINE
(In the Accademia delle Belle Arti, Venice)

There is, perhaps, no other religious subject which has so often stimulated the inspiration of the great Italian painters. Veronese himself has treated the same scene several times. The painting here reproduced is considered, in view of the picturesqueness of its composition, the beauty of the faces, and the brilliance of the colouring, to be one of the best works of the illustrious artist.

THE VISION OF ST. HELENA
(In the National Gallery, London)

This picture has often been attributed to Zelotti, who was a friend and at one time a collaborator of Veronese. But the composition, the colouring, the finish of detail, and the sumptuousness of decoration betray the hand of the immortal author of the *Wedding at Cana*.

CRESCENT MOON PUBLISHING

web: www.crmoon.com e-mail: cresmopub@yahoo.co.uk

ARTS, PAINTING, SCULPTURE

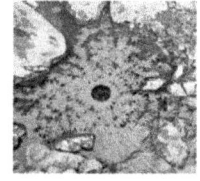

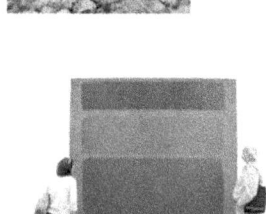

The Art of Andy Goldsworthy
Andy Goldsworthy: Touching Nature
Andy Goldsworthy in Close-Up
Andy Goldsworthy: Pocket Guide
Andy Goldsworthy In America

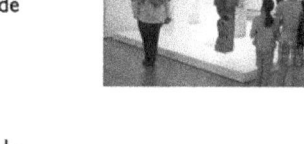

Land Art: A Complete Guide
The Art of Richard Long
Richard Long: Pocket Guide
Land Art In the UK

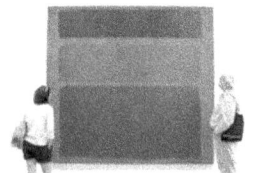

Land Art in Close-Up
Land Art In the U.S.A.
Land Art: Pocket Guide
Installation Art in Close-Up
Minimal Art and Artists In the 1960s and After
Colourfield Painting
Land Art DVD, TV documentary
Andy Goldsworthy DVD, TV documentary
The Erotic Object: Sexuality in Sculpture From Prehistory to the Present Day
Sex in Art: Pornography and Pleasure in Painting and Sculpture
Postwar Art
Sacred Gardens: The Garden in Myth, Religion and Art
Glorification: Religious Abstraction in Renaissance and 20th Century Art
Early Netherlandish Painting
Leonardo da Vinci
Piero della Francesca
Giovanni Bellini

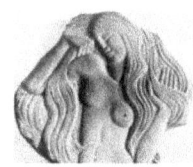

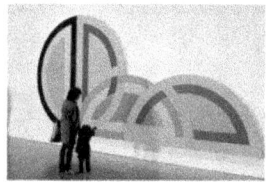

Fra Angelico: Art and Religion in the Renaissance
Mark Rothko: The Art of Transcendence
Frank Stella: American Abstract Artist
Jasper Johns
Brice Marden

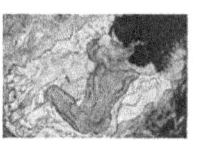

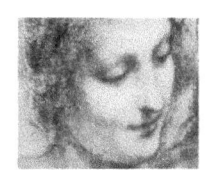

Alison Wilding: The Embrace of Sculpture
Vincent van Gogh: Visionary Landscapes
Eric Gill: Nuptials of God
Constantin Brancusi: Sculpting the Essence of Things
Max Beckmann
Caravaggio
Gustave Moreau
Egon Schiele: Sex and Death In Purple Stockings
Delizioso Fotografico Fervore: Works In Process 1
Sacro Cuore: Works In Process 2
The Light Eternal: J.M.W. Turner
The Madonna Glorified: Karen Arthurs

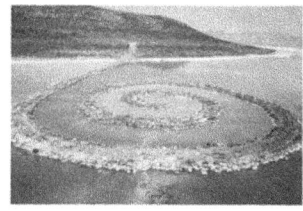

LITERATURE

J.R.R. Tolkien: The Books, The Films, The Whole Cultural Phenomenon
J.R.R. Tolkien: Pocket Guide
Tolkien's Heroic Quest
The *Earthsea* Books of Ursula Le Guin
Beauties, Beasts and Enchantment: Classic French Fairy Tales
German Popular Stories by the Brothers Grimm
Philip Pullman and *His Dark Materials*
Sexing Hardy: Thomas Hardy and Feminism
Thomas Hardy's *Tess of the d'Urbervilles*
Thomas Hardy's *Jude the Obscure*
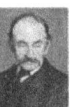
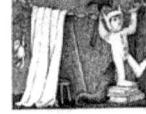
Thomas Hardy: The Tragic Novels
Love and Tragedy: Thomas Hardy
The Poetry of Landscape in Hardy
Wessex Revisited: Thomas Hardy and John Cowper Powys
Wolfgang Iser: Essays and Interviews
Petrarch, Dante and the Troubadours
Maurice Sendak and the Art of Children's Book Illustration
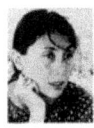
Andrea Dworkin
Cixous, Irigaray, Kristeva: The *Jouissance* of French Feminism
Julia Kristeva: Art, Love, Melancholy, Philosophy, Semiotics and Psychoanalysis
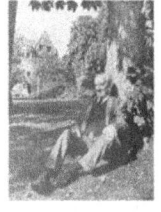
Hélène Cixous I Love You: The *Jouissance* of Writing
Luce Irigaray: Lips, Kissing, and the Politics of Sexual Difference
Peter Redgrove: Here Comes the Flood
Peter Redgrove: Sex-Magic-Poetry-Cornwall
Lawrence Durrell: Between Love and Death, East and West
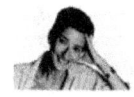
Love, Culture & Poetry: Lawrence Durrell
Cavafy: Anatomy of a Soul
German Romantic Poetry: Goethe, Novalis, Heine, Hölderlin
Feminism and Shakespeare
Shakespeare: Love, Poetry & Magic
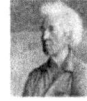
The Passion of D.H. Lawrence
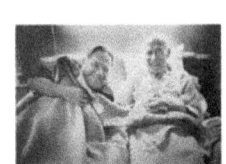
D.H. Lawrence: Symbolic Landscapes
D.H. Lawrence: Infinite Sensual Violence
Rimbaud: Arthur Rimbaud and the Magic of Poetry
The Ecstasies of John Cowper Powys
Sensualism and Mythology: The Wessex Novels of John Cowper Powys
Amorous Life: John Cowper Powys and the Manifestation of Affectivity (H.W. Fawkner)
Postmodern Powys: New Essays on John Cowper Powys (Joe Boulter)
Rethinking Powys: Critical Essays on John Cowper Powys
Paul Bowles & Bernardo Bertolucci
Rainer Maria Rilke
Joseph Conrad: *Heart of Darkness*
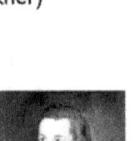
In the Dim Void: Samuel Beckett
Samuel Beckett Goes into the Silence
André Gide: Fiction and Fervour
Jackie Collins and the Blockbuster Novel
Blinded By Her Light: The Love-Poetry of Robert Graves
The Passion of Colours: Travels In Mediterranean Lands
Poetic Forms

POETRY

Ursula Le Guin: Walking In Cornwall
Peter Redgrove: Here Comes The Flood
Peter Redgrove: Sex-Magic-Poetry-Cornwall
Dante: Selections From the Vita Nuova
Petrarch, Dante and the Troubadours
William Shakespeare: Sonnets
William Shakespeare: Complete Poems
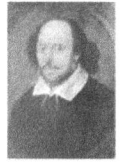
Blinded By Her Light: The Love-Poetry of Robert Graves
Emily Dickinson: Selected Poems
Emily Brontë: Poems
Thomas Hardy: Selected Poems
Percy Bysshe Shelley: Poems
John Keats: Selected Poems
Joh n Keats: Poems of 1820
D.H. Lawrence: Selected Poems
Edmund Spenser: Poems
Edmund Spenser: Amoretti
John Donne: Poems
Henry Vaughan: Poems
Sir Thomas Wyatt: Poems
Robert Herrick: Selected Poems
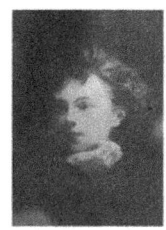
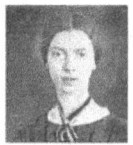
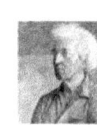

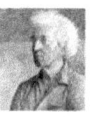
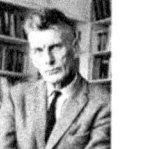
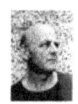
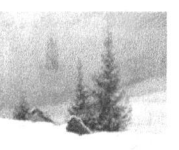
Rilke: Space, Essence and Angels in the Poetry of Rainer Maria Rilke
Rainer Maria Rilke: Selected Poems
Friedrich Hölderlin: Selected Poems
Arseny Tarkovsky: Selected Poems
Arthur Rimbaud: Selected Poems
Arthur Rimbaud: A Season in Hell
Arthur Rimbaud and the Magic of Poetry
Novalis: Hymns To the Night
German Romantic Poetry
Paul Verlaine: Selected Poems
Elizaethan Sonnet Cycles
D.J. Enright: By-Blows
Jeremy Reed: Brigitte's Blue Heart
Jeremy Reed: Claudia Schiffer's Red Shoes
Gorgeous Little Orpheus
Radiance: New Poems
Crescent Moon Book of Nature Poetry
Crescent Moon Book of Love Poetry
Crescent Moon Book of Mystical Poetry
Crescent Moon Book of Elizabethan Love Poetry
Crescent Moon Book of Metaphysical Poetry
Crescent Moon Book of Romantic Poetry
Pagan America: New American Poetry
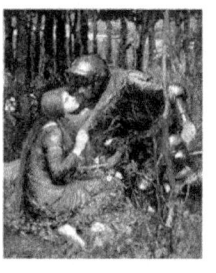
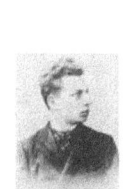
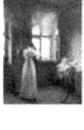

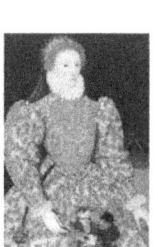

MEDIA, CINEMA, FEMINISM and CULTURAL STUDIES

J.R.R. Tolkien: The Books, The Films, The Whole Cultural Phenomenon
J.R.R. Tolkien: Pocket Guide
The *Lord of the Rings* Movies: Pocket Guide
The Cinema of Hayao Miyazaki
Hayao Miyazaki: *Princess Mononoke*: Pocket Movie Guide
Hayao Miyazaki: *Spirited Away*: Pocket Movie Guide
Tim Burton : Hallowe'en For Hollywood
Ken Russell
Ken Russell: *Tommy*: Pocket Movie Guide
The Ghost Dance: The Origins of Religion
The Peyote Cult
Cixous, Irigaray, Kristeva: The *Jouissance* of French Feminism
Julia Kristeva: Art, Love, Melancholy, Philosophy, Semiotics and Psychoanalysis
Luce Irigaray: Lips, Kissing, and the Politics of Sexual Difference
Hélène Cixous I Love You: The *Jouissance* of Writing
Andrea Dworkin
'Cosmo Woman': The World of Women's Magazines
Women in Pop Music
HomeGround: The Kate Bush Anthology
Discovering the Goddess (Geoffrey Ashe)
The Poetry of Cinema
The Sacred Cinema of Andrei Tarkovsky
Andrei Tarkovsky: Pocket Guide
Andrei Tarkovsky: *Mirror*: Pocket Movie Guide
Andrei Tarkovsky: *The Sacrifice*: Pocket Movie Guide
Walerian Borowczyk: Cinema of Erotic Dreams
Jean-Luc Godard: The Passion of Cinema
Jean-Luc Godard: *Hail Mary*: Pocket Movie Guide
Jean-Luc Godard: *Contempt*: Pocket Movie Guide
Jean-Luc Godard: *Pierrot le Fou*: Pocket Movie Guide
John Hughes and Eighties Cinema
Ferris Bueller's Day Off: Pocket Movie Guide
Jean-Luc Godard: Pocket Guide
The Cinema of Richard Linklater
Liv Tyler: Star In Ascendance
Blade Runner and the Films of Philip K. Dick
Paul Bowles and Bernardo Bertolucci
Media Hell: Radio, TV and the Press
An Open Letter to the BBC
Detonation Britain: Nuclear War in the UK
Feminism and Shakespeare
Wild Zones: Pornography, Art and Feminism
Sex in Art: Pornography and Pleasure in Painting and Sculpture
Sexing Hardy: Thomas Hardy and Feminism

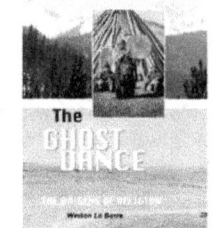
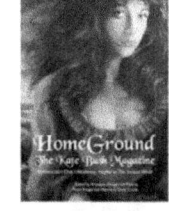
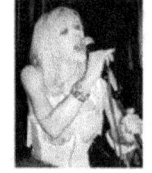
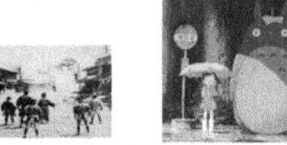
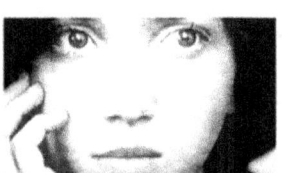

The Light Eternal is a model monograph, an exemplary job. The subject matter of the book is beautifully organised and dead on beam. (Lawrence Durrell)
It is amazing for me to see my work treated with such passion and respect. (Andrea Dworkin)

CRESCENT MOON PUBLISHING
P.O. Box 1312, Maidstone, Kent, ME14 5XU, Great Britain. www.crmoon.com

cresmopub@yahoo.co.uk   www.crescentmoon.org.uk